a beautiful pain

A MOTHER'S GRIEF JOURNEY

LEANNE DAVIDSON

God is just so much love

Leanne

Print ISBN 978-1-7382502-0-2

Cover photo credit: Madelyn Copperwaite and emPowerPR Group

This book is dedicated to my sons, Davis and Mikael, hearts of my heart.
Davis, you are my kind, compassionate, steady rock.
Mikael, you are our shining star and we miss you more than words can describe.

Without love, there will not be grief but without love there will also not be life.

The depth of our grief is the depth of our love; it is infinite.

— LEANNE DAVIDSON

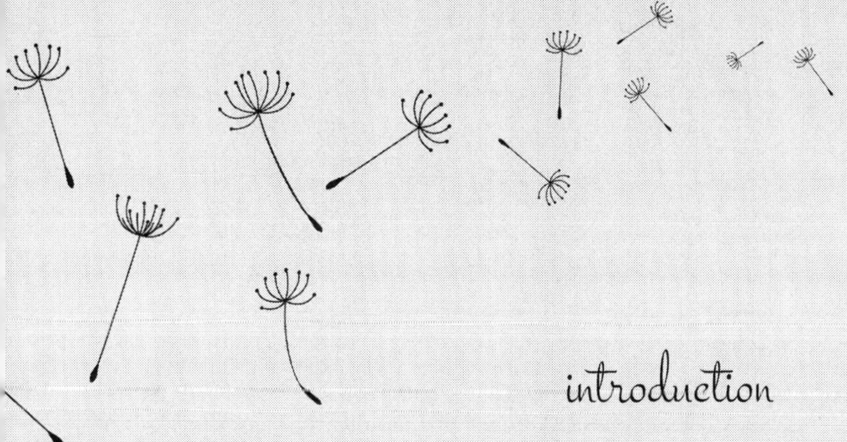

introduction

If you are reading this book, it is likely that you, like me, have lost a child, or you love someone who has and want to know more about their grief journey. I wrote this book to share my journey of grief with others hoping they may find understanding and compassion from a fellow sojourner.

To put the ideas and feelings expressed in this book into perspective, I thought it would be helpful to tell you a bit about who I am and how I came to be here.

I was born into a Christian family and my parents were both, in my opinion, quite amazing. My dad was a commercial fisherman, and our family spent a lot of time outdoors and on the lake. It really was an idyllic childhood, which, like many of us, I didn't realize until later in life. My mom was gentle and kind and an absolute prayer warrior. My parents taught me and my siblings to love the Lord and to live with honesty and integrity.

My sisters Lynda and Shannon, my brother David, and I have been incredibly blessed to be able to call Stuart and Shelagh Longe "Mom" and "Dad." They have both passed away and are with the Lord; Dad in 2017 from cancer and Mom in 2023 due to complications from dementia. We miss them dearly.

When I was at university in my twenties, unfortunately, I happened to meet a man who I thought was a Christian but who turned out to be something entirely different. I ended up in an abusive marriage I was only able to escape from with the help of my family and close friends. The few years I spent in this horrific relationship had a profound effect on my faith. I knew throughout the experience that God loved me and was with me, and the process of becoming free of the abusive marriage strengthened my faith tremendously.

In my late twenties, I found myself on my own with two children. My son Davis was a toddler and Mikael a baby. As a single mom, the parenting was all up to me; the boys and I lived our way forward with a lot of love for each other. There were a lot of mistakes, a lot of laughter, a lot of fun, and sometimes a lot of heartache. In other words, it was messy and glorious! I love being a mom, and my sons have blessed every part of my life. We also have a large extended family; between myself and my three siblings there are fourteen children, so that means lots of cousins!

The one area of my life I struggled to let God control was in relationships, and I made many mistakes that were not what God had planned for me at all. Then one day as I was driving home, I prayed and told the Lord I didn't know what I was doing. I was placing my life and all relationship matters fully into his hands. I was forty-seven years old; I guess I was a slow learner!

God must have been waiting patiently for me because shortly after my prayer, he brought my husband, Tim, into my life. We had known each other for years and as young people had attended youth group together. It really was like a storybook romance, and I have so much gratitude for God's gift of a wonderful husband. Tim is smart, funny, kind, thoughtful, and loves me to pieces! We were married in 2009—when Mikael was eighteen and Davis nineteen—and Tim has been my supporter through the past fourteen years of marriage. He has been a wonderful support to both the boys, and their relationship has been very loving and positive.

Such a positive relationship was a blessing for all of us as Mikael was struggling with addiction. He began this struggle in high school and by his mid-twenties, he was battling the disease of addiction to opioids. He was in Vancouver at the time and came home to Kenora, Ontario—about 150 miles north of Minnesota—to begin the process of trying to get clean and sober. He knew he needed his family's support.

Mikael worked hard on his twelve-step program and over the next six years had short relapses between long periods of time where he was clean and sober. Our family became even closer as we supported Mikael and learned more about the disease he was battling. Over the summer of 2022, I could see such positive spiritual growth in Mikael. He was doing so well, and I had such hope for his future.

And then on November 27, 2022, my world as I knew it was shattered by a phone call telling me that my son Mikael was gone from this world. He was thirty-one years old and his death ripped my heart into pieces and completely wiped out everything I thought I knew or understood.

As a Christian mother, one of the things I *did* know was that I needed God to carry me and hold onto me; I simply could not walk this new path alone. One of the things God prompted me toward was to write my thoughts and feelings as a way of processing what was happening to me. This didn't happen overnight. It took me a while to start writing.

But, in the end, I found it helpful to put my thinking in concrete form. Through encouragement from a number of friends and family, I felt led to compile my journal entries and put them into a book I hope is helpful to other parents.

You will see as you follow my journal entries that the journey of grief is not a linear one but one full of ups and downs, curves and circles, clarity and confusion, pain and hope. There were times when the only way I could find to express my feelings was in a poem, so these are embedded in my journal along the way. It is now my hope that sharing my grief experience may in some way help you if you are living in the "After" as I am. If you are supporting someone who is living in the After, you may also find it helpful as you try to understand and help them.

This book is an outpouring of my thoughts, feelings, ponderings, and realizations over the first eight months after Mikael died. As you read it there may be parts where you think, "Yes, that's exactly how I feel," and other parts where you think, "I don't feel that way at all." And that is so completely okay! This book is not meant to dictate what anyone else's grief should look like. I believe that as individuals who are unique and special, we each experience grief in our own unique way.

I have found it incredibly helpful to connect with other parents on the same journey as I am. This is my way of continuing to connect with grieving parents so we can find understanding and support through this heartbreaking, agonizing, and collective journey.

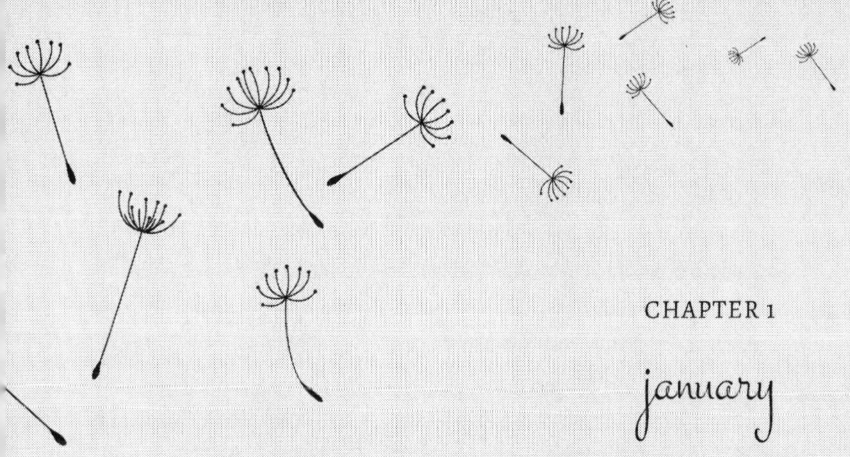

CHAPTER 1

january

JANUARY 6: THE AFTER

There is no way to explain the before and after to anyone who has not experienced it. When we are living in the "Before," we have no idea that there could ever be an After. We are living our lives, making plans with confidence in them coming to fruition. In my Before, Mikael was clean for the past six months, and I was so hopeful he was going to make it this time. We were becoming even closer, and I would hear from him regularly. He texted and called; we had lunch together; he would stop by the office, come out to visit, and spend time with all of us as a family. He would often share his spiritual growth and experiences as he worked through his steps and faith in God. He asked me for my advice often and was interested in my faith journey and in sharing together. He had just been hired in a new job working with youth that he would have been amazing at.

I had gone to Thunder Bay, about five hours away, to be with my mother, who was having hip surgery. She had dementia and needed to have a family member with her to help with decisions and just be there with her. I was planning on meeting a friend for supper in Thunder Bay and then, just like that, I was tumbled into the After.

A phone call from Davis. Absolutely impossible words to accept or believe. The After. There is no returning from it. In my Before, we had plans. Plans for a trip, plans for retirement, plans for dinner, plans. In my After, those plans seem fleeting, uncertain, not to be trusted.

We find our way through the After and learn how to live in it. It is the never-ending nightmare where each morning when we wake up, we have to realize again that it is our reality. It is another earthly realm that no one but God can help us traverse.

Each morning in my After, I wake up and think *Mikael*. Then the wave of reality hits, like a train. Then I plead, "Lord, help me," and he answers every day: "Yes, I will. I am with you."

JANUARY 12: A SHATTERING

It is so very hard to describe this pain of losing my son. There is no "moving on," "getting over it," or "complete healing." It is the absolute shattering of my heart in a way that the pieces cannot be glued back together—much like the shattering of a teacup. You can attempt to glue it back together all you want, but the end result will be missing gaps and cracks; it will never be the same.

I think God picks up all those pieces of my heart and helps me to carry them forward in my life, just as they are. I believe he holds those pieces as sacred and belonging to him, so he will protect them and also use the pieces of my heart to help others as I continue through life, fully trusting him.

I so often feel completely empty of everything. Empty of feelings, empty of motivation, empty of thoughts. It's like there is a cavern inside my body. I wonder if it will eventually fill with something—but with what? It makes me think I need to be so vigilant about whether this emptiness gets filled and how it gets filled. Maybe it just goes away with time. I honestly don't know.

JANUARY 16: CHRISTMAS

Mikael loved Christmas. So do I. The decorating, getting a tree, baking, family time, carols, ice candles, snow; we love it all. I knew this Christmas I needed to honor Mikael and celebrate as he would want me to. So, I threw myself into Christmas and thought about Mikael with every activity that I did. I decorated the house for the season, and we went out with my son Davis and his family and found a wonderful Christmas tree. I baked the cookies we all love and the homemade turtles, and of course the cinnamon buns! We played Christmas music often.

Tim and I spent time with both our families on Christmas Eve, Christmas Day, and Boxing Day. We spent time on Christmas morning watching our granddaughters open their gifts, and having Christmas morning breakfast together was peaceful and joyful in so many ways.

Throughout the entire season I could feel the absence of Mikael like a stone in my stomach, and I know the rest of the family could feel it too. As I am now taking down decorations and putting things away, I know I will do it all again next year. Though there is great pain in celebrating Christ's birth without Mikael here, I believe that for me to do otherwise would be even worse. Not celebrating Christmas would not make his absence feel better. And so, I will continue to celebrate this favourite season of mine and Mikael's each year because I know he would want me to.

JANUARY 20: MORNINGS

I find mornings the hardest. The second my eyes open, my heart and brain cry out, "Mikael." It seems easier to go back to sleep—the only time my brain is not thinking about Mikael. At least, that I know of. Mornings are a daily, repeated smashing of my heart. It takes time to prepare myself, and I have to go through routines of prayer, Bible reading, coffee, and relaxation in order to be able to get up and move forward into the day.

I try to give myself one task to do each day, just to get me up and going. Especially on weekends when work doesn't require me to get up. I could lay in bed all day, and I worry about depression setting in. How will I even know when grief has turned into depression? Would I feel the shift? Would my husband feel it in me? I hope so.

For now, I try to make myself do one thing: change the water filter, complete a craft, do the dishes, go for a snowshoe, take down the Christmas decorations, etc., etc. Even if it is a task that only takes a few minutes, it makes me get up and do something.

JANUARY 26: HELPFUL WORDS

When you lose one of your children, there are many things friends and family will say to try to help. How difficult it is for them to even begin to find the right words. Even when things said are awkward, I must remember they are said in love, and that's all that matters.

A very good friend said something to me that I found extremely helpful because it was so real. When I said I didn't always know how to go on, she said that I would because I didn't have a choice. How true! So honest and real. I do not have a choice; my life will continue with or without my full mental and emotional participation. It is a choice I make every day to ask Jesus to be with me for that day and to help me go into the day trusting him with my steps.

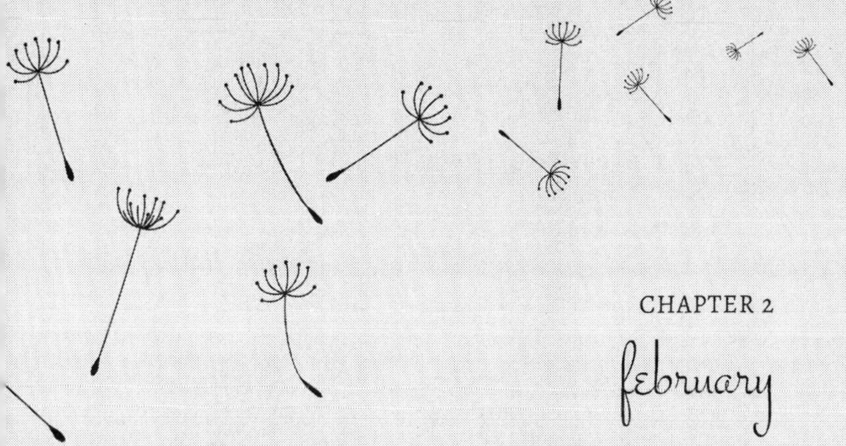

CHAPTER 2

february

FEBRUARY 11: WAVES

I have heard people say that grief comes in waves. I certainly experienced that this week. It was such a difficult week for no particular reason. I found myself completely raw and unable to cope with simple situations. When this happens, I've realized it's best to just let it be instead of trying to fight it and "pull myself together." It's hard to be around other people when these waves hit because it seems impossible to interact. These are days when I find it better to be by myself.

When I'm feeling this, I do a lot of talking to God. And listening. And letting God surround me. Matthew 28:20 says, "And surely I am with you always, to the very end of the age."

FEBRUARY 12: A BEAUTIFUL PAIN

How can pain be beautiful? As I contemplate the love I have for my sons, it is clearly so incredibly immense and everlasting and unconditional. It is a beautiful love. Because I love them so much, the pain I am feeling now from losing Mikael is an equally beautiful pain. It is pain felt because of the beauty of great love.

There are so many levels of grief that seem impossible to find words to express. I love Mikael and Davis with every piece of my body. I will always love them. Mikael is not here anymore, but that doesn't stop my love. If there are those who think that over time, my love will fade and this will get easier, they are wrong. Every mother knows that our love for our children never fades or dissipates—whether they are with us or not. I will love Mikael for the rest of my life with the same fierceness. I carried him in my body, and he is part of me. I am part of him. We are connected forever.

FEBRUARY 13: WHAT IS MIKAEL DOING?

The other day I was talking to my granddaughter about Mikael and about him now being in heaven with God. It's a hard concept for a four-year-old to wrap her brain around. She asked, "What is he doing there?" and I found myself thinking, "Good question! What *is* he actually doing?" So, I went to my Bible and did some research, and this is what I came up with.

First of all, Mikael has a new body, and he has been transformed. He has no pain or sadness.

"But our citizenship is in heaven. And we eagerly await a Savior from there, the Lord Jesus Christ, who, by the power that enables him to bring everything under his control, will transform our lowly bodies so that they will be like his glorious body" (Philippians 3:20-21).

"Dear friends, now we are children of God, and what we will be has not yet been made known. But [...] when Christ appears, we shall be like him, for we shall see him as he is" (1 John 3:2).

The second thing I found were several verses that gave me a glimpse into Mikael's current heavenly activities.

- He is worshipping the Lord.

"Then I heard every creature in heaven and on earth and under the earth and on the sea and all that is in them, saying: 'To him who sits on the throne and to the Lamb be praise and honor and glory and power, for ever and ever!" (Revelation 5:13).

- He is feasting and eating with the Lord and his people.

"On this mountain the Lord Almighty will prepare a feast of rich food for all peoples, a banquet of aged wine—the best of meats and the finest of wines. On this mountain he will destroy the shroud that enfolds all peoples, the sheet that covers all nations; he will swallow up death forever. The Sovereign Lord will wipe away the tears from all faces; he will remove his people's disgrace from all the earth. The Lord has spoken" (Isaiah 25:6-8).

"'I say to you that many will come from the east and the west, and will take their places at the feast with Abraham, Isaac and Jacob in the kingdom of heaven'" (Matthew 8:11).

- He is living together with other believers and being reunited with loved ones.

I love to think of him being reunited with my dad. What joy for them to see each other.

- He will celebrate for eternity.

"Then the angel said to me, 'Write this: Blessed are those who are invited to the wedding supper of the Lamb!' And he added, 'These are the true words of God'" (Revelation 19:9).

- He is serving the Lord in any way the Lord asks him to.

It's important that Christ himself said we are to serve the Lord and that he was serving God. We are to serve the Lord here on this earth and will continue to serve him in heaven. The Bible doesn't tell us much about what that constitutes "in heaven," so I suppose I can only speculate about the kinds of things Mikael may be doing in service to God. I do know that the angels serve God in many different ways—for example, acting as messengers. I don't really have to know the specifics of what God will ask of Mikael in his new, transformed body; I just need to know that Mikael is useful, fulfilled, happy, glorious, perfect.

"Whoever serves me must follow me; and where I am, my servant also will be. My Father will honor the one who serves me" (John 12:26).

- He is appreciating the absolute beauty of heaven.

Revelation 21 and 22 provide descriptions of heaven. I imagine the difficulty of describing in words the vision of heaven the writer of Revelations had. But it is clearly a beautiful place, far surpassing the beauty of this earth. I imagine Mikael being in awe of the beauty surrounding him.

FEBRUARY 14: AIRPORT

I went back to work about three weeks after Mikael died. I felt like I needed to be busy, and staying home all day alone with my fragmented and fragile heart and thoughts seemed like a bad idea for me. So, I gradually returned, and for the most part, the work has helped me to at least develop a routine that allows me to function.

Part of my job includes travel to Toronto at times for various meetings. In January, I had to make my first trip since losing Mikael, and I wasn't sure how it would go. I knew once I was there, in a small group meeting, I would be okay because I would be with people I knew and who supported me.

It worried me to be away from home and my husband, to be actually travelling— the drive to the airport, being in an airport, and then a plane surrounded by strangers who know nothing about me. What if I lost my composure? What if I broke down? Sobbing uncontrollably in my hotel room is one thing, but having a breakdown in the middle of an airport is an entirely different experience I didn't want to have. Anyway, I made it through the trip, and it felt like a small accomplishment of some kind.

When I was in the airport on my return home, waiting for my luggage, I looked around at all the other passengers. My initial thought was that I was surrounded by all these people who knew nothing about what I was going through. They knew nothing about the ache in my soul or how much energy it was taking me to hold it together and appear normal to everyone. But the next thought I had was that I also had no idea what any of them were going through or feeling. What if one of them had lost their job or received a terrible medical diagnosis or was going through a divorce or had lost a loved one?

From the surface, there was no way for me to tell. It really brought home to me the point of Christ's command to love one another as he loves us. The new buzzword today is "be kind," and it is such a simple concept that really struck me that day standing at the luggage carousel. We have no idea what anyone we come across in our day-to-day travels is dealing with. Kindness, patience, and helpfulness are so important. It is challenging me to be more aware and do my best to show Christ's love to others.

FEBRUARY 15: DISTRACTION

The other day, I came out of a meeting about my mother and tried to get into my vehicle. It took me a moment to realize that it wasn't my vehicle. In fact, my vehicle wasn't even parked close to it! Oh dear! What I think is even funnier is that this has happened multiple times over the past few weeks.

Distraction! This is what it looks like. My mind is distracted with the constant underlying thoughts surrounding Mikael. Distraction. Repeating tasks because I don't remember doing them, or not doing a task because I think I already did it. Distraction!

I'm sharing this because you may be experiencing this same distraction if you are struggling with difficult circumstances. You are not alone, and you are not losing your mind! It can be rather disconcerting, but I think it's completely normal. I think it will eventually pass—hopefully before I am arrested for attempted car theft!

Along with distraction, of course, comes brain fog. Those of you who have or are experiencing menopause know exactly what I'm talking about! Just amplify it by ten or one hundred times, depending on the day. I'm not a grief expert by any means, but I definitely know that right now, my brain is not functioning the same as it was before. I'd like to say I'm a pretty intelligent woman, and so it is rather unnerving to find myself forgetting things, searching for words, being unsure of information that I should be certain of, and second-guessing myself at every turn. I do believe this will pass over time.

FEBRUARY 16: NECESSARY TASKS

Today I have to go to the doctor's office to get paperwork filled out for the bank. Mikael had a loan with life insurance on it, so this is a necessary procedure. This is a part of loss no one talks about. I wasn't prepared for the necessary tasks that result from losing someone you love so dearly: a letter from a lawyer, dealing with bank accounts, gathering paperwork for income taxes, etc. I have an envelope with death certificates sitting in my vehicle in case I need them. It feels so cold, clinical, impersonal. I hate having to think about and deal with these things, but it must be done. These tasks seem to have nothing to do with who Mikael was—his heart and soul.

I did have a bit of a chuckle the other day when I received mail "to the estate of Mikael Baranyi." Estate! For those who know Mikael, that would consist of his clothes and his golf clubs! His real "estate" was the richness of his friendships and the love and acceptance he spread to others wherever he went.

One of the tasks I still have to do is to go through his things. I find myself partly hesitant to do it because of the emotional toll and partly wanting to do it so I can immerse myself in the things he touched, held, and wore—except his socks. I don't want to immerse myself in his socks!

Mikael used to leave his socks all over the house! You would find socks in the kitchen, on the dining room floor, in the bathroom, on the couch, hanging over a chair. They never matched! Similarly, half-filled cans of pop or sparkling water could be found randomly scattered around the house or yard, wherever he happened to leave them and forget about them. So, when I am sitting at the doctor's office to complete this task of paperwork, I will think about Mikael's socks!

FEBRUARY 18: IF I COULD JUST

There are times I find myself wishing, "If I could just..."

If I could just hug Mikael one more time.
If I could just talk to him one more time.
If I could just tell him how special he is one more time.
If I could just tell him I love him one more time.

But there is no "one more time." There is no time. So, I have to think about how I will accept this and how I will go forward with it. The thoughts of "If I could just" are dangerous for those who are grieving. They so easily lead to "If I had only," "I should have," "Why didn't I?" On the path of grief, sinking into thoughts like these is like throwing yourself off a cliff and having to climb it again. The past cannot be changed, and grief causes enough pain without getting trapped in it.

So, what I have come to is this: Mikael knew I loved him, and he knew I thought he was special. The last time we talked, it was good and positive, and we both gained something from our conversation. Our last hug was the last time we saw each other because he hugged me all the time. I can hang on to all those times and close my eyes and imagine them whenever I find myself thinking, "If I could just." I can keep Mikael alive in my soul with all the memories I will always have.

Sharing those memories with others helps me keep him present and real. And it is important to me that he is real to others and not forgotten. It is important that I let my friends know I want to talk about him and I want to share who he is. I want to laugh at the things he would laugh at and the things he did that were funny. There were many. I want to share his philosophies with others because they were so thoughtful and perceptive. I want to share his accomplishments, and I want everyone to see how amazing he is.

FEBRUARY 20: STAGES OF GRIEF

We have all heard of the stages of grief from counselors, authors, psychologists, etc. Some describe five stages of grief, and some describe seven. The five stages of grief are described as: Denial, Anger, Bargaining, Depression, Acceptance. The seven stages of grief are described as: Shock, Denial, Anger, Bargaining, Depression, Acceptance and Hope, Processing. I personally like the seven-stage description best.

These stages do make sense, and I know each person is individual in the ways they experience and process their grief. I think these stages are guidelines we need to be aware of, but they are not meant to be boxes we put ourselves into as we strike out on the most difficult journey of our lives.

I also think the stages of grief are leaving out a very

important element, which I call the God Factor. God experienced tremendous grief when his Son, Jesus Christ, died on the cross for our salvation. He understands our grief. He is also our creator and knows us intimately and completely. If we are walking in a relationship with Christ, then we have the absolute champ of a counselor at our fingertips 24/7. Not only is God there for us throughout all the stages or feelings we experience, but he is able to comfort, guide, and direct us in what we need to do each moment to help ourselves in this process. He will carry us, if needed, and use us to assist others.

There are times when my existence feels so forlorn and broken. When I can barely move or think past my brokenness. But still, God is there in those moments. He is the air around me, the voice in my ear, saying, "I love you. You are mine. I will carry you."

FEBRUARY 22: THE PAINTING

Last week, we were at Davis's place visiting. He brought me a wrapped package and told me it was a late Christmas gift from Mikael. He told me it was an idea that Mikael had for a Christmas gift for me and that he had been really excited about it. When I opened the package, it was a painting of my dad. It was from a photo taken of Dad driving the boat on a day he and Mom had taken Tim and me out fishing. It had been such a great day. My heart was a puddle.

Davis told me Mikael had been planning this, and since

he wasn't able to complete the plan, Davis did on his behalf so I would have his gift. There are no words for me to express the amazing heart both my sons have.

Later on, I thought about how Mikael would have been planning this gift and talking to Davis about it. Just weeks before he died, he was planning special Christmas gifts. He was also planning to start a new job and was excited about it. It seems so unfathomable that shortly after, he would be gone.

This is the thing about losing one of your children. It is never expected. It is never from natural causes. It is always some kind of unexpected tragedy; an accident or an illness. It creates an added layer to our grief because it all seems so unthinkable. There are many days I just cannot get my head to fully grasp that Mikael is not here. These days especially I must hand over to the Lord, because they are days of frozen inability to function. Only God can carry this, so I choose to let him.

FEBRUARY 23: DAY BY DAY

There are days when my heart feels like a stone. I can't feel anything, and I move through the day in a bit of a daze. There are other days when my emotions are so close to the surface, I can barely contain them. Some days, I claw through bit by bit. Other days, I feel like I'm managing. There are still other days when I feel joy in life, in my family, and in my surroundings. There are days I laugh and days I cry.

I know God is with me in all these moments, even when I'm faltering. When I feel his presence and when I don't. Psalm 139:7–10 says, "Where can I go from your Spirit? Where can I flee from your presence? If I go up to the heavens, you are there; if I make my bed in the depths, you are there. If I rise on the wings of the dawn, if I settle on the far side of the sea, even there your hand will guide me, your right hand will hold me fast."

FEBRUARY 24: MIKAEL'S NOTES

Mikael used to have a whiteboard in his room, and he would write down things that encouraged, challenged, or motivated him.

Gratitude—Something he always tried to practice, even when things went wrong.

God will steer, but God won't row.—Mikael knew he needed God to steer the boat, but he also knew we are expected to do the work too. In Philippians 3:14, Paul says he is striving towards the goal "to win the prize for which God has called me heavenward in Christ Jesus." We need to be actively working through our faith. I do think there are times when God helps us row when we need him to. In fact, there are times when we need God to take over the entire boat!

The road less travelled—I think this was on Mikael's board because he was challenged to go outside his comfort zone.

Live with your heart, not your head.—Mikael definitely lived with his heart. He touched so many people and made them feel special.

What beautiful creatures we are. See the light. See the good. It's here if you look for it.—Mikael was able to see the good in others.

Pray for the people you're mad at.—Wise words from my son!

Look for opportunities for growth from bad situations/circumstances, morally or other.—This is something Mikael really strived to do. Regardless of what was happening to him, good or bad, he would so often relate to me what it was teaching him about himself and how it was helping him grow as a person.

What can I learn today? Who can I help today? Who can I love today? Set aside what I thought I knew.—If we all started our day with these four goals, imagine what our world would be like!

FEBRUARY 26: TO WHOM SHALL WE GO?

Of all the characters in the Bible, Peter is one of my favorites. A fisherman, a working man, sincere, impetuous, heart on his sleeve. His flaws were right out there, and as a flawed individual myself, I can really relate to him. He loved Jesus with his whole being!

In John chapter 6, Jesus is with the disciples shortly after the feeding of the five thousand. Jesus had clearly stated that he was the bread of life, and many of the disciples stopped following him. Jesus asked the twelve disciples if they also wanted to leave, and Peter says, "'Lord, to whom shall we go? You have the words of eternal life. We have come to believe and to know that you are the Holy One of God'" (verses 68–69).

To whom shall we go? There it is! No matter our circumstances, there is not a time when we do not need the Lord. To whom shall we go? We shall go to the Lord. As I think about Mikael each and every day, I cannot think about him without also being aware that God is right beside me in my memories and thoughts.

One of the things I think about often is that many friends and family have said Mikael was a bright light in this world. I think about his brightness, and I am challenged to strive to be the same—to ask God to help me to continue sharing brightness and light wherever I go.

FEBRUARY 27: PICTURES

Over the weekend, I was going through boxes of family photos from my parents. I have been sorting them and scanning as many as possible onto a hard drive so my siblings and I can each have a copy of pictures of Mom and Dad and the fourteen kids between us.

It was so bittersweet going through pictures of the kids. So many happy times with Mikael and his cousins. Looking at pictures of him laughing and having fun made me smile and cry at the same time. It is so hard to move my mind from all the joy in the pictures to the current reality of Mikael's absence.

Today, it has been exactly three months since he died. It feels like three days and forever at the same time. I will keep going, one day at a time. These pictures will be precious to me as they allow me to see him at all ages, smiling and happy. I could sit and look at his sweet face all day.

FEBRUARY 28: LAUGHTER

Mikael had the best laugh ever! Room-filling, explosive, joyful! When Mikael laughed, you just wanted to laugh right along with him, even if you didn't know what he was laughing at! There are just some people who have the most infectious and distinctive laughter. My dad also had a great laugh. You could find him in a crowded room just by listening to him laughing.

When we were kids, we went as a family to the theatre. Back then (I'm aging myself) there were cartoons that played before the feature film. Dad would sit in the theatre and laugh out loud at the cartoons. We thought that was so funny! My brother David also has a great laugh, and it's a lot like Dad's.

Over the past few months, whenever I find myself laughing at something, I am a little surprised inside but also relieved. Surprised, I guess, that I am able to laugh and relieved that I am still able to feel joy and humour. I suppose when others hear me laughing, it may cause them to think I must be doing better and "moving on." This, of course, is not the case. My heart is still broken, but grief doesn't preclude laughter or joy. Thank the Lord for that. Although there are certainly days where I feel completely wooden, there are also days where I feel the full breadth of my emotions, laughter included.

Mikael laughed often, and I know he would want to hear me laughing and finding joy in the world around me. And I will.

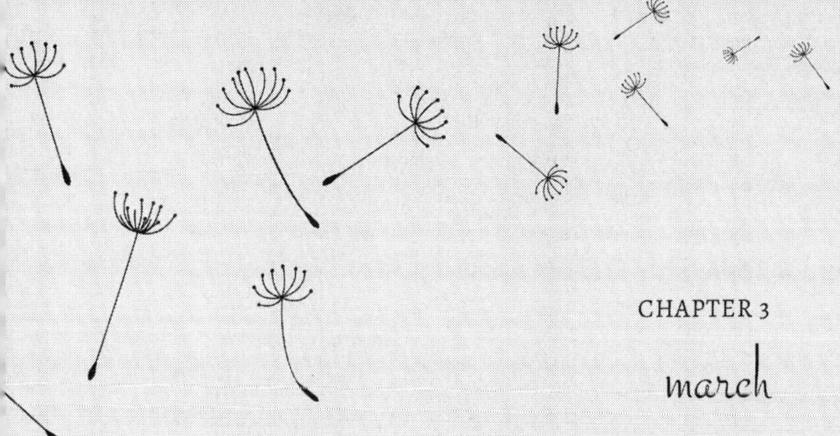

CHAPTER 3

march

MARCH 2: THE REMEMBERERS

I saw a post on Facebook the other day that really caught my eye. It was about being the "Rememberers"—those who are left behind but keep the memories of loved ones alive and share them with others. The Rememberers share stories so they don't get lost over generations. What a wonderful word, Rememberers! I don't know who wrote the post, but I would love to be able to tell them how profound it was.

Being a Rememberer is an honour and a serious commitment. I am a Rememberer for my dad and for my son, Mikael. I am not alone in this task, and I have many friends and family who also take on the role. It is important to note when bereaved parents such as myself regularly talk about our child and our grief, it is not to draw attention to ourselves, but rather to ensure our child is never forgotten. To ensure the stories about who they were continue on and their names are not left in the past.

To be a Rememberer is not to pretend those we are

remembering are perfect people with no flaws. It is to embrace everything about them and then to focus on the very best of them and share those memories.

I will take Mikael with me in my heart and in my thoughts and with my words for as long as I am in this world. I will be his Rememberer.

MARCH 3: SOCIAL EXHAUSTION

Last night, I had a work dinner at a local restaurant. It was a good dinner, and it was not a late night, and yet I was so exhausted afterwards. This is not the first time I have felt wrung out from a social event.

What everyone sees on the surface is me taking part in conversations, talking, laughing, and seeming "normal." But within my brain there is a division of thought and effort on two separate planes. On one plane, I am paying attention to others in conversation and taking an active part; on the other, I think wholly of Mikael. You see, he is on my mind all the time, and I can't change that. It takes a lot of mental effort to socialize with others.

So, if at a social event you see me phase out momentarily, it's not because I don't enjoy the event or your company. I'm just regrouping.

MARCH 5: WINGS OF EAGLES

I woke up in the middle of the night last night, and my immediate thought was of Mikael. I started to pray and asked the Lord for help and comfort. I closed my eyes, and I could see the silhouette of an eagle with wings outstretched, soaring. The eagle's body wasn't feathers; it was sky and trees and sunlight. It was beautiful, magnificent! The message for me was that Mikael is soaring on the wings of eagles. All is well with him. Thank you, Lord.

MARCH 7: MUSIC

I love music and listen to it every single day. I have a lot of favourites, but there are also certain songs that just hit a chord with me whenever I hear them. I find that music aligns with our situations and feelings in such a profound way and often says what we cannot.

Choosing the music for Mikael's funeral was so important to me. I wanted the songs to be meaningful to him and also to our family. Mikael's good friend, Dan, helped me find songs for the service for which I am very grateful. I still can't listen to "Come As You Are" by Crowder or "No Longer Slaves" by Zach Williams without crying throughout.

Yesterday, as I was purchasing and downloading new music into a playlist, I came across an artist I had not heard of before. I'm sure there are those of you who have heard of her. Her name is Lauren Daigle, and I found a song she sings called "Rescue" that simply brought me to my knees. The power and beauty of her voice and the message of the lyrics are heart wrenching.

Her song reminded me that God always hears me and sees me. He hears what we say "under our breath" that we don't want anyone else to hear. God knows our innermost thoughts and pain and fear. He can and will rescue me. He can and will rescue you.

I know God rescued Mikael. And I'm sure there will be those who might wonder how I can believe that when Mikael died. How did God rescue him? But God's promise of rescue isn't about us never physically dying. It is about saving our beings, our essence, our souls and bringing us home to safety and healing. God saw Mikael. He heard him. God rescued him.

Music is a powerful part of our lives. I will listen to this song repeatedly and cry and feel hope and comfort and assurance. If you have favourite songs, I encourage you to listen to them often and to share them with your friends and family.

MARCH 8: SOME DAYS WILL BE LIKE THIS

It's International Women's Day. Well, this woman will need a lot of grace today. I've been up since four a.m., not able to stop the wheels turning or shut down my brain. It's going to happen, and some days will just be like this. I don't see it as steps forward or backward but just a reality of loss and all that is part of it. So, today, I will just be. I will just let God's grace carry me today.

MARCH 9: A GIFT

I received a rough-hewn granite bench as a gift yesterday from a group of friends. I was so incredibly touched, literally brought to tears. So thoughtful and generous. It is such a beautiful reminder of Mikael, and I have already started planning exactly where in our garden it will go. This poem is etched in the seat:

I thought of you with love today, but that is nothing new.
I thought about you yesterday and days before that too.
I think of you in silence. I often speak your name.
All I have are memories and your picture in a frame.

Your memory is my keepsake with which I'll never
part.
God has you in his keeping. I have you in my
heart.

The line in the poem about having only memories and pictures in a frame really struck me. I spend a lot of time looking at pictures and videos of Mikael. It is never enough! I keep wishing I could reach into a photo and pull him out of it! But as the poem says, these frozen snapshots of time are all we physically have left. That, and our memories we hold closely around us.

While I'm gardening this summer, I can stop and rest on this bench. I can stop and just be. And think of my memories and hopefully smile.

MARCH 10: ON THE SURFACE

This weekend I am at the annual general meeting for my teacher's union. As the unit president, I am also the head of delegation. So, I have to be present. I find myself moving through the day, talking, laughing, holding down conversations, acting like I'm fine. Sometimes I wonder if I'm leading people to believe I *am* fine. Do they think, "Wow, she's really doing great! She's sure moving on." I'm not, of course. But what else can I do? If I stop functioning, my grief will still continue. If I stop socializing, my grief will still continue. Life will continue around me whether I participate or not.

I think this is part of God helping me to function and to take part in the life going on around me. I think, exhausting as it is, I gain strength and hope from taking part. Because there are a lot of good things to take part in. And yes, there will still be times where I will lock myself away and collapse and hide for a time. But God will find me there. God will always find me.

MARCH 12: MUSIC 2

Music is so important in my grief journey—all kinds of music. Music that reminds us of them. Music that allows us to feel and connect and let our emotions out. I listen to songs that remind me of Mikael all the time, and for some reason, the music helps me to let my emotions flow.

Music that allows us to have fun is also important on this path. I was at our annual general meeting for work not long ago, and on Sunday night there was a party with a live band. My husband had come to join me for the evening, and we spent hours dancing and having fun. (Yes, I said it —having fun! It is okay to have fun while you are grieving, in case anyone thought they weren't allowed.) The time we spent on the dance floor was such a reprieve from everything. The music allowed us to escape our thoughts, feel the beat, and just let loose. It may have only been for a few hours, but spending time this way is so important because it takes us out of our heads.

Opportunities to get out of my inner thought process are important, and I need to embrace them when they occur —with intentional balance. We can't do this all the time, or we would never be in touch with our grief—and that would be detrimental to our health. However, in balance, finding these moments provides us with mental rest, reminds us of who we are as people, and allows us to enjoy the life we are still living.

MARCH 16: THE DOG

We are spending a week in Mexico, and I have been thinking so much about Mikael here. Obviously, I think about him constantly, but my memories here are somehow different—more relaxed, if that makes sense.

I recalled a funny incident he and I experienced on one of our trips here. We stayed in Puerto Aventuras, and from the resort you could arrange transport to this well-known jewelry store that was popular with tourists. When we were waiting for the return van after doing our shopping, the friendliest dog approached our group. Tail wagging, bum wiggling, he greeted all of us, and as typical North Americans we all responded, "Oh, what a cute puppy!" as we all petted him affectionately and repeatedly.

Our van approached, and we all climbed on and got settled. It took only a few seconds for a group reaction as the van pulled away. What is that putrid smell? It was the most horrific, disgusting, overpowering odor! We realized it was coming from us, from our hands. The dog! We rolled down all the windows and hung out our heads. Mikael and I laughed and laughed—and ran to wash off the second we reached the resort!

MARCH 18: BEACH THOUGHTS

Sitting on the beach looking out at the ocean gives you a lot of time to think. Sometimes that's good, sometimes that's not so good, and sometimes it just is. Yesterday while sitting and looking at the waves, I thought about too many things to write down today. One of the things I found myself pondering were the mistakes I made as a mother and how they affected Mikael. I thought about how long it took me to forgive myself for those mistakes but how quickly Mikael was able to forgive me. I told him once that it was okay to be angry with me, but he would have none of it. From conversations with others and with Mikael, I know that he saw me through a lens of the strongest love and affection. I was his mamma!

Sometimes as parents, we think about how fiercely we love our children and forget how much they love us. Yesterday, I really thought about the power of Mikael's love for me. Not just his love for me, but also Davis's and Tim's and my family and friends'. I thought about how much I am loved and what a blessing from God it is. The love I receive here in this world is what helps me function each day.

MARCH 20: MEANDERING

It's difficult sometimes—many times—to put into words what is happening in my thoughts on this journey. It's a journey like none I've ever been on before. When I was a kid, we did this art exercise where you randomly drew all over a blank page without lifting your pencil and then colored in the sections that were created. This is a bit like how this journey feels—random. There are days where I think I'm managing and maybe I'm getting somewhere (where do I think I'm getting?), and days where I just can't absorb what has happened.

On those days, it feels like everything is so elusive. I think about Mikael not being here, and I can't grasp it as a concrete thing. My brain can't settle around that reality. It's like trying to catch bubbles in the air; they just pop if you manage to touch them. On these days, I just hang on and wait. Sometimes that is all you can do, and that is okay.

MARCH 22: GOD'S UNDERSTANDING

When Christ died on the cross, there was an earthquake and the temple curtain—which was extremely thick and heavy—was torn in two (Matthew 27:51). I see this as an incredibly powerful sign of God's intense grief and agony as Jesus died for us. Imagine agony so great that its power causes an actual earthquake! I also recognize the symbolism of the curtain being torn as representing us no longer being separated from God, as Christ's death has provided us with a way to directly access God. But still, I think God's grief and agony were also demonstrated in a very physical way. It helps me to know that God truly does understand the depth of my grief. He also felt it. I don't think there is anything we could feel that God has not felt and does not understand.

MARCH 24: ADDICTION

It is tempting to avoid this topic, but for me, part of my grief process includes being the mother of a son struggling with the disease of addiction. I might not have touched upon this part of my life very much, but I realize there may be others out there who are going through this, and it may help them to know they are not alone.

Being the parent of an addict is a very difficult road for one to travel. As a mom, I emotionally went through the hills and valleys with Mikael as he fought this battle. I hoped when he was in recovery and rejoiced at seeing him make positive steps and beginning to feel so good about himself. I despaired when he relapsed and endured the pain of knowing how much he was hurting and how badly he felt about himself during those times. I felt absolute terror for his well-being and safety—a terror that was always just below the surface and never truly went away entirely. I felt frustration at the disease and its devastating effects.

As the mom of an addict, I had to learn a lot of hard truths about myself along the way. I had to analyze my reactions and motives and work on my own personal growth. It was important to know when my approach was hurtful and to own it and apologize.

It was also important for me to set healthy boundaries to allow our relationship to grow in a positive way. Sometimes holding the line on those boundaries was very, very, difficult. Saying no to your child whom you love so dearly does not come naturally to a mother.

Being the parent of an addict can come along with a great deal of guilt. We analyze our parenting and constantly wonder if any of our actions were part of the cause. Being a parent, period, comes with guilt. I believe guilt is one of the most damaging and unproductive emotions, and it must be dealt with so you don't drown in it. It is an ongoing process of understanding that we are human and flawed but not to blame. These are two separate things. We can own our mistakes and work on ourselves without guilt—with God's help.

Being the mother of an addict also comes with the hurt of listening to other people's comments about addiction. It can mean hearing the others' judgement of "those addicts," and it hurts to the very core. It includes getting useless and thoughtless advice from those who have no idea what it is like to walk in these shoes. But it also means having friends and family who surround you and your son with support and love and are there for you always. You learn quickly who you wish to remain close to and who you need to keep your distance from.

If you are the parent of a child with the disease of addiction, I hope you know that you are not alone. I hope you can reach out and surround yourself with the friends and family who will support you in the ways you need so you don't walk the road alone. And I hope you take God along with you on this road, as it really can't be traveled without him.

MARCH 26: THE IN-BETWEEN

I sometimes feel caught between two realms. One is here with my family. I love them and I know they need me to be in their lives, and I want to be in their lives and experiences. The other realm is where Mikael is and where I also long to be. It is a realm I can't be in right now, and yet I find myself yearning to be there with Mikael. To be clear, this is not a feeling of wanting to die at all, just a yearning to be in two places; one with my family here, and one with Mikael.

I also often wonder if Mikael can see us, and I believe he can. It comforts me to think he can see us with love from where he is. Not long ago, I read an opinion that argued our loved ones could not see us from heaven because heaven is a place where there is no pain or sorrow, and they couldn't possibly see us without those feelings. I find myself disagreeing with this opinion because it doesn't take into account the fact that our bodies and minds are transformed when we are in heaven. We are not the same as we are here on earth. So, I think it is entirely possible to be in heaven and able to see our loved ones on earth and to not feel any pain or sorrow.

1 Corinthians 13:12 says, "For now we see only a reflection as in a mirror; then we shall see face to face. Now I know in part; then I shall know fully, even as I am fully known." This is how I believe Mikael can see us: from a perspective of knowing fully.

MARCH 28: WAVES

Mikael really liked a song called "Waves" by Dean Lewis. I think he really connected with it, and the lyrics hit home with how I think he often felt. I listen to the song often and usually cry as I do. It is a beautiful song, and I feel Mikael all around me when I listen to it.

Yesterday was exactly four months since he's been gone. It feels like four days, four years, four minutes. I continue to long for him to walk through the door. He is on my mind when I'm driving, in a meeting, doing the dishes, going for a walk, in a conversation—you get the picture. One of the things I've found is that if I engage in an activity that requires a lot of concentration, like a carpentry project, a puzzle, or a sewing project, my mind has to focus on the task, and I have a period of time where I think only of that task. It provides a bit of a reprieve or a mental rest, which when you are grieving is much needed. I've completed a truckload of puzzles!

MARCH 31: TIME

There are just some days where I look at the vast cavern of time between now and when I will see Mikael again, and I can't grasp it. It seems so far, like I can't even come close to touching it. There are days where my grief sits right in my throat. So fragile. Like I will disintegrate if I even move. Where do I end up on these days? I end up at the foot of the cross, because where else can I go? I don't know any other way to move through my life except in the arms of God. I didn't know any other way before I lost Mikael, and I don't know any other way now.

This part of my grief is something I really struggle with because the concept of the time between now and when I will see Mikael again is overwhelming. If I get caught up with contemplating it for too long, I end up adrift. So, at the foot of the cross where I find myself each day, I pray and ask God to help me break time down to just one day. Just one day.

The concept of "one day at a time" is certainly not a new one. Mikael practiced this in his twelve-step program as well. There are also many verses in the Bible, such as Matthew 6:34, that encourage us to focus on today and not worry over tomorrow. As a grieving parent, I find I am forced to live this way: one minute, one hour, one day at a time.

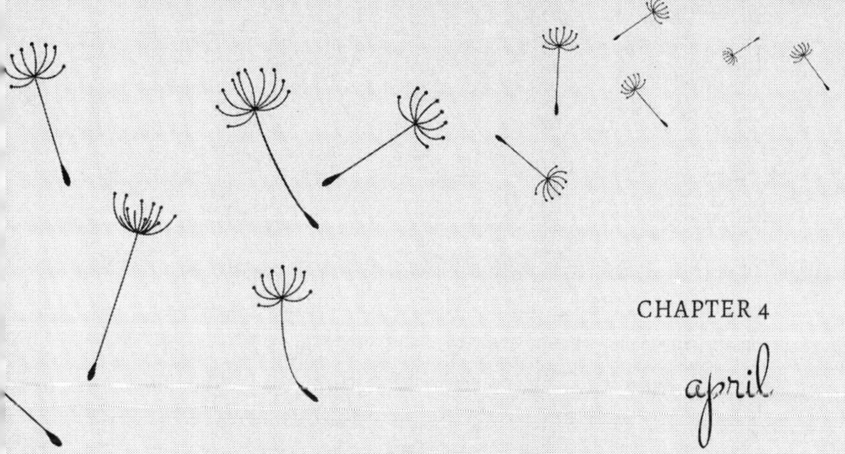

CHAPTER 4

april

APRIL 3: HOW ARE YOU DOING?

One of our most common North American greetings is "Hey, how are you?" "How are you doing?" "How's it going?" I know I have said a version of this to many people over the years. Now it feels like a trick question. How *am* I doing? Hmm. The real answer would take a while to express. If I say "okay," then you may think I actually am okay. What does "okay" mean, anyway? Does it mean all is good, or does it mean I am still standing and coping with life?

It is a trick question! Even with my friends, who I know really care about me and want to know how I am, it feels like a trick question. I don't have an answer. But I also know they are asking out of love and concern, so I answer the best I can.

The funny thing is that I probably still say, "How are you?" as a greeting to others! I have been trying to be more aware of this and find other ways of greeting friends and acquaintances. One of the greetings I find helpful to say instead is "So nice to see you."

APRIL 5: GRATITUDE

I feel the need to express how thankful I am for all the friends and family who support me. There have been so many amazing people who have been alongside me over the past four months. My husband has been such a rock and, despite his own grief, has been solidly there for me and ready to comfort. So many friends and family members check in on me and accept me in whatever state they find me in. My son Davis and his family have been such a blessing, and time spent with them has helped me in too many ways to express.

I know it can be difficult to feel like you know what to do or say when you have a loved one who is going through deep grief. I have been there myself when I've had friends who suffer loss. What I have learned through this is that it doesn't matter what words you say; it just matters that you are there. Whether it is a phone call just to check in, a text or email to say, "I love you and I'm thinking about you," going out for a coffee, an invite for dinner, etc. You don't need to come up with fancy words, and there aren't *any* words that can change anything—but your presence does. If you are supporting a friend in grief and feeling inept at it, please be assured that if you are there, you are helping.

APRIL 7: THE FLIP SIDE

I have been spending a lot of time lately just thinking about how much I miss Mikael and how much I wish he were here. My focus has been on missing him, and there are so many days where I still feel unable to grasp that he is simply no longer here. I keep trying to make this concept concrete in my mind, and it seems like trying to hold water in my hands.

Yesterday, I was just sitting and thinking, and I started to wonder how things might change for me if I flipped the focus of my thinking from where Mikael *isn't* to where Mikael *is*. Mikael is with God and in a place where he is healed, joyful, purposeful, and transformed. Trying to imagine what heaven is like as a location is also rather like holding water in your hands, but I know it is a place so wonderful it brings me a sense of calmness and reassurance to know Mikael is there.

Refocusing my thinking hasn't made me miss Mikael less, of course, but focusing on the knowledge that he isn't aimlessly floating around out there somewhere but is in a marvelous and incredible place comforts me.

APRIL 9: WHAT WE LEAVE

On Friday I picked up all of Mikael's things and brought them home to sort through. I have been putting this off for months because, for one thing, it felt just too hard, and for another, it felt like a cold and clinical task I didn't want to do. The process has sent a gazillion different feelings through me, and I'm not totally sure I will be able to unravel them all.

While I was sorting through his things, our little Jack Russell, Millie, came into the room and when she smelled his clothes she started wriggling and wagging her tail. She was so excited because she absolutely adores Mikael and thought he was here. My heart splintered just watching her and her confusion about why she could smell him and not find him.

The smell of him. I would take one of his sweatshirts

and just hold it up to my face and breathe him in. I kept one of his sweaters out that he often wore just so I could smell him and feel closer to him. One of the thoughts I had as I sorted through things was how could his life come to this: boxes of clothing, golf clubs, shoes, a few tools. Is this what is left? As I think about Mikael, I realize this is not so. The people he touched with his kindness and understanding, his humor and ability to light up a room, his determination, his acceptance of others—this is what is left. Mikael's legacy is about all the people's lives that he touched and made better. It's the testimony from so many that he helped them, encouraged them, and made them feel special.

None of the things we leave behind will ever matter. But the results of our actions will continue to live on afterwards. I can only hope I will leave a legacy of kindness and acceptance as strong as Mikael's. I miss you, Mikael, with every breath I take.

APRIL 11: BROTHERS

Davis and Mikael were two peas in a pod. They were more than brothers; they were best friends. They looked out for each other and were a big part of each other's lives. The boys were nineteen months apart, so they did everything together growing up and formed a close bond and friendship based on knowing each other better than anyone else ever could. They had many adventures together and definitely had each other's back. Of course, as siblings, they still had those down and dirty, knockout fights! It used to boggle my mind how one minute they were pounding on each other and ten minutes later could be happily shooting hoops, riding their bikes down the road, or playing Xbox.

This brotherhood and friendship was based on knowing the best and worst of each other, accepting all of it, and loving each other fiercely. Mikael would tell anyone who asked that Davis was the best older brother a person could hope to have. He looked out for Mikael and helped him out many times. He was a constant in Mikael's life, and Mikael told me many times how Davis's steady presence helped him. I really want to honour Davis and his love for Mikael and the depth of the grief I know he is carrying.

APRIL 13: UNEXPECTED MOMENTS

The other day I went through all of Mikael's things and sorted them. It was both painful and cathartic at the same time. Some of his clothing was stained and ripped because he had worn them to work (he worked for his cousin's construction company), so I put them in a separate box to deal with later and put the box outside by the garage.

Yesterday, as I was pulling my vehicle around in the driveway to head to work, that box was sitting there, directly in my line of sight. And just like that, I couldn't breathe. This box, so forlorn. What was I thinking? Why did I put it there? Why did I separate his things? How is this okay? How is he gone, and this is what's left? Why couldn't he hold on? Why? Why?

I cried all the way to work. These moments seem to come out of nowhere, and there is no other way to proceed than to go through them. I can't go around, ignore, or push them away. I have to go through. Yesterday, that meant I clawed my way along with all the rawness it entailed. On days like this, I will claw my way until I can get onto my knees to crawl, and then I will crawl until I can stand up and walk. The next time I find myself facedown and unable to breathe, I will do it all over again. This is grief.

APRIL 14: FURTHER THOUGHTS ON MEANDERINGS

The other day, I described grief like the artwork I remembered doing as a child in school. We were given paper and pencil and then just drew free-form all over the page, the only rule being to not lift the pencil until we were done. I don't see my grief journey as linear, but I think many often do. It's not a straight line or even a jagged line with ups and downs. It is a continuous, interconnected pathway. I don't work through a feeling and then never return to it. I work through the same feelings again and again, and each time it looks a bit different.

Just like the artwork I did as a child, I can color in one section at a time with my own style and personality. I can fill in the sections of my life with the things I choose to spend my time on—like time spent with family, helping others, enjoying nature, reading, and just sitting in the sun! I can fill in the sections with memories of Mikael and with what I learn as I just keep living.

APRIL 17: A DIFFERENT ME

I have just started trying to process the partial loss of my identity. I am not the same person in many different ways, and I can't always even pinpoint how I'm different; I just know that I am. This is an additional loss, and it is also part of the process of grief I am going through. Because I am part of Mikael and he is part of me, when he left it felt like he took parts of me with him. It's really difficult to explain this aspect of loss.

Before Mikael died, I knew myself very well. I was a very reflective person and very in-tune with my strengths and weaknesses. In this After I am now in, I am finding that parts of me are not the same, and I am still trying to figure out this new person. My reactions to things are not always what I would normally have expected, and so I have to re-reflect, so to speak, in order to figure out and get in tune with this new me. There are certainly still parts of the old me here, and I'm not sure anyone else would notice that I am different, but I definitely notice.

This process includes feelings of the loss of who I was and learning to embrace who I am now. A verse that really helps me is Psalm 139:13–16, which says, "You created my inmost being; you knit me together in my mother's womb. I praise you because I am fearfully and wonderfully made; your works are wonderful, I know that full well… Your eyes saw my unformed body; all the days ordained for me were written in your book before one of them came to be." God knows every part of me: the old me and the new me. I am loved in all forms.

Part of the new me is a person who carries sadness in my soul that I did not carry before. As I am learning to accept this, I cherish every moment of joy—and there are many if we seek them out. Joyful moments do not remove the sadness, but they make it easier for me to carry it.

APRIL 19: ABOUT MIKAEL

I want to share a bit about Mikael today. Since photos tell a good part of a story, here is Mikael in action!

He loved fishing and golf and spent a lot of time with good friends enjoying these pastimes.

Physical fitness was important to him, and he enjoyed the challenge—and even more, the camaraderie with friends at the gym.

He was funny and fun! Mikael was never worried about how he looked. He just enjoyed time with people, embraced silliness, laughed at himself, and was fun to be around.

His smile is worth a gazillion bucks!

APRIL 22: PRESENCE

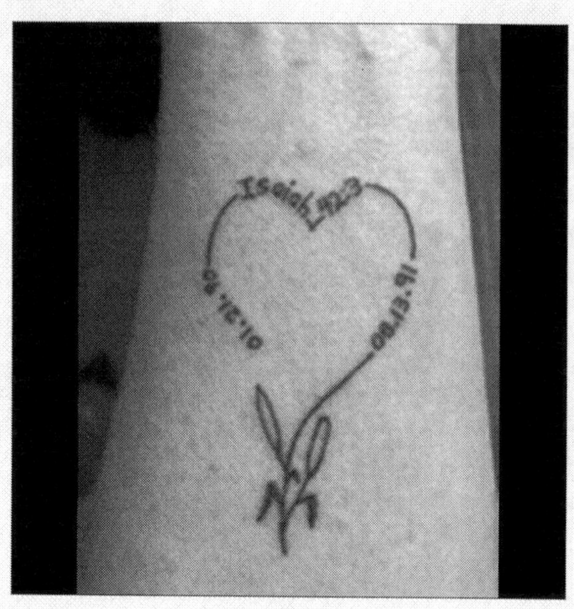

This is a tattoo that I have on my arm so that I can see it every day. It includes Davis's and Mikael's birthdates and a verse that was special for Mikael and me. The verse is Isaiah 42:3, which says, "A bruised reed he will not break, and a smoldering wick he will not snuff out." I sent this verse to Mikael to remind him that God would honor his striving. I could feel Mikael so close to me the whole time I was getting the tattoo and every time I look at it.

I find myself trying to reach out to every tangible thing I can to keep some form of Mikael's existence here. I constantly look at photos and watch videos. I wear the bracelet I gave him as a gift. The tattoo is a constant, visible reminder of both of my sons. I wear Mikael's old pants and shirt around the house. I saved one of his sweaters without washing it because it smells like him. It is like trying to take all the invisible threads that connect us and make them visible. Make them touchable, feelable, real. Because Mikael can't just be a memory; he has to be here somehow. I am instinctively surrounding myself with every possible physical sign of his presence.

APRIL 23: A DAY FOR PRAYER

The other day, I attended a professional development day at one of our schools and sat in a presentation on family-centric learning. Shortly after the speaker was introduced, she told us she was going to start with a short slideshow. She had titled her slide show "The Mother." I felt a twinging in my brain, a bit of a warning signal that I didn't recognize at first. The slideshow started, and as pictures of the mother and son went across the screen, I could feel my tears begin and my heart collapsing. I quickly left the gymnasium—though it could better be said that I fled.

There were two other mothers in the audience who were also grieving the loss of a child. They each left the gym shortly after I did. The three of us sat together in a quiet office and spent the rest of the presentation time sharing with one another and supporting each other. I simply cannot say in words how powerful this was for me and how much it meant to be able to be with these two amazing moms and know we did not have to try to find words to explain anything to each other. I realized how important it is for us to stay in contact with one another and check in on each other. As I connect with other grieving parents, I can tell you they are the most amazing, strong, heroic people I have ever met.

Later that afternoon, after I had gone home, I received a call telling me one of the parents in our school system had been in a car accident. Neither of her children had survived. I could feel her massive pain and shock. I wanted so badly to physically reach out through time and space and hold onto her. I spent most of the night praying for both parents and asking God to send angels to them. There are no words for the shattering they are experiencing, and I hope those of us who are living in the After with them can offer them love and support.

APRIL 24: FORGIVENESS

Because of the way Mikael died, the police have kept some of his belongings for their investigation. I find myself having difficulty with the possible end result of an investigation. If the individual who sold Mikael the fentanyl was eventually charged and faced prison time, there are probably those who would consider this justice and believe it should bring me some sense of peace. It will not.

Although I recognize that justice is necessary, it isn't something that will change anything for me. I don't think Mikael would want punishment for this person either. I already have a pretty good idea of who the individual is, and what I really want is for them to have a different life. I want them to know that God loves them. That they are forgiven. That they can change their life by handing it over to God and choosing a relationship with Christ. This is what I want and what I know Mikael wants for this person. The justice system cannot do this for them. Only God can, if they choose to let him. And so, this is my prayer for this person.

APRIL 25: FORGIVENESS PART 2

My husband and I had a conversation last night about forgiveness. Our perspectives were different and equally valid. Tim's struggle was more to do with people being responsible for the wrong they do, such as the dealer who sold Mikael drugs potentially knowing they were a lethal dosage. My perspective is more to do with how forgiveness affects me internally. It made me think about all the levels of forgiveness that are part of our lives.

Forgiveness can be as simple as accepting an apology when someone accidently bumps into us and spills our groceries on the ground. Forgiveness can be about forgiving our friends or family for things said or done that were hurtful. Forgiveness is part of our lives, and it is necessary for relationships to continue in a loving and healthy way. Forgiveness is what Christ offered us by dying on the cross and by triumphing over it. Forgiveness is the cornerstone of our salvation and of our lives. Forgiveness is necessary if we are to move forward in our lives in any kind of positive direction. Forgiveness does not hinge on the atonement of others; it is separate from another's capacity to acknowledge wrong.

For me, forgiveness also means forgiving the person who sold Mikael the drugs that killed him. It means forgiving myself for not physically being there when Mikael was in the process of relapsing. It means forgiving myself for the past and for not taking us out of a living situation that was hurtful to him because I was "trying to make it work." It means forgiving his biological father who, years ago, offered him drugs and contributed to his addiction. My husband, Tim, and I are still working on forgiving him, and we are just not there yet.

Forgiveness is massive. It is an instrument of change. It

is one of the most important actions we can do for ourselves, for our family, and for the world around us. Forgiveness changes our hearts, our perspectives, and our trajectory in this world. Forgiveness is what I continue to work on for myself and for others. God challenges me to dig deep and find his path to forgive.

APRIL 27: GUILT

Guilt and motherhood—where to start? It can seem like a battle for our peace sometimes. When our kids are little and we're just starting out, we so often wonder, "Am I doing it right?" So many incidents and scenarios can have us second-guessing if we are good moms or not. That includes little things like snapping at them when we're tired and rushed and bigger things like when we wonder how our decisions have affected them. It makes me think how important it is for older moms like me to encourage younger moms.

Guilt and motherhood and grief is an even more difficult combination. I don't know what others' experience is with feelings of guilt while grieving, but I know I have sometimes had to deal with these feelings over the past five months. Feelings of guilt come in waves and can't be anticipated, as they can be triggered out of seemingly nowhere. They are like the unwanted guest who arrives unexpectedly; sometimes they just stay for a coffee, and sometimes they come with a suitcase for an extended stay.

My hardest guilt hurdle is thinking about times when Mikael felt like he wasn't good enough. Being in a relationship with someone who has the disease of addiction involves some very difficult conversations and responses. Although you're both doing the best you can with what you know, there are just times in our humanness where we do or say hurtful things. Every time I think of an instance where Mikael felt like he wasn't good enough, I can't bear it.

Most of the time, I know Mikael knew how much I loved and cherished him and how proud I was of him. Once in a while, though, that unwelcome visitor, guilt, steps in and makes me worry there were times he didn't. My heart breaks into pieces. Guilt is destructive and will break us down. It has to be faced and dealt with.

I don't know how others deal with guilt, but I have to allow myself to feel it rather than stuffing it away. I have to hurt through it and acknowledge it. Then I look to God's Word and God's reminders to me of what is actually rational and true, and I am able to emerge from it. God's Word tells me that self-forgiveness is as important as the forgiveness of others. God reminds me of his grace and shows me all the ways I am a good and loving mother. I am reminded that Mikael did know I loved him and that he was enough.

APRIL 29: TO MIKAEL

Darkness and Light
One hides
One reveals what's hidden
Your life was light
fighting the darkness

Pain and Joy
One crushes inwards
One explodes outwards
Your life was joy
emerging from your pain

Sorrow and Love
One is a result
One is the reason
Love cannot be had
without sorrow

It is the price we pay
I will pay it
to love you
with my entire being

CHAPTER 5

may

MAY 1: MORE ABOUT MIKAEL

Sharing about Mikael is one of my favorite things to do! So, here are some things about him that you may not have known.

That boy loved a bath! My word, he *loved* soaking in the tub! Mikael would come over for a visit, and for the first half hour or so, we wouldn't even see him. He'd come in the house, head to the bathroom, draw a bath and soak in it, then join us for a visit. He especially loved the jetted tub; he would be disappointed that I've replaced it with a non-jetted one.

Mikael brought his own food with him everywhere he went. Heading to the gym? Make sure you have a container of rice or noodles in your gym bag for before and after. Coming over for dinner? Arrive with leftovers, eat them an hour before dinner, and then eat dinner too! Road trip? Mikael was like a magician, pulling all kinds of food out of his bag en route; which, of course, means *you* have to drive to enable his snacking! Along with food, he also had an endless supply of carbonated water with him at all times.

Tupperware could not be trusted in Mikael's care. When he came over for dinner, if he was taking leftovers home with him, you had to be aware and accept that you would never see your containers again. *Ever!*

For as long as I can remember, Mikael wore two different socks. He never paired them up—just grabbed two socks out of the drawer and put them on. At one point, I noticed this had become a fad; I had to smile. He also left his socks lying around the house wherever he happened to be when he took them off. Socks could be found under the kitchen table, in the bathroom, or on the stairs, but rarely in the laundry basket.

Mikael wasn't one for reading fiction. He was much more interested in researching a topic or watching a documentary and then sharing what he learned with you. He did a lot of reading when researching information about a person or topic that piqued his interest. He also loved movies and was a very talented actor himself. Tim and I always enjoyed having Mikael over for a movie night.

Mikael was just a really special person, and I miss him every moment of every day.

MAY 2: THANKFULNESS

In church on Sunday, as we were singing, I was struggling with my emotions. I often cry during the worship music, so this was nothing new. As I was standing there, I noticed a plaque on the wall right in front of me with the following verse on it: "Rejoice always, pray continually, give thanks in all circumstances; for this is God's will for you in Christ Jesus" (1 Thessalonians 5:16–18). I did not feel overly thankful at that moment. I stood there wondering how I could be thankful in this circumstance. How can holding all this sorrow be something to be thankful for? But as I continued looking at the verse, I realized that is not really what it was saying.

Of course God does not expect me to be thankful for Mikael's death or for the sorrow I carry. The verse doesn't say to be thankful *for* your circumstances, but to be thankful *in* them. In this new, immensely painful path I am on, God has provided much for me to be thankful for.

I am thankful for the assurance I have that Mikael is with the Lord, safe and healed. I am thankful for my husband, Tim, who has been so supportive and loving. I am thankful for Davis, for the wonderful son he is and for how much joy he brings into my life. I am thankful for my daughter-in-law, Carollyn, and her kindness and love. I am over the moon in love with my granddaughters. I am so very thankful that I am able to retire this year, as I know I cannot continue doing my job and need to be able to move on to other things. I appreciate where I live because the country setting is so peaceful for me, and I need the peace that sitting looking out over the lake can bring.

The reality is that I will continue to carry sorrow with me no matter what. Whether I choose to live with bitterness and anger or to live with thankfulness, I will carry that sorrow. It seems to me I would rather carry that sorrow in the light than in the dark. So, working on having a spirit of thankfulness makes sense to me. I know I will have days when I struggle to be thankful and stray down that dark path, and those will be days when I trust God's grace to hang onto me and lead me back.

MAY 4: OPEN WATER

Over this past week, the ice has been melting on our lake. As it does every year, it started with the ice blackening and breaking away from the shore. This honeycombed ice sounds like chimes as the wind blows it and breaks it apart. The eagles appear and sit on this thin ice, watching for fish. The ice disappears quickly at this point, and the day when the lake is open water shining in the sun is one of my favourites.

The eagles take their leave and are replaced by seagulls. Seagulls remind me of children on the playground. As a group, they are in continual fluid motion. I can hear them playing, calling out to one another, the odd squabble!

This week, I have sat on the deck and looked over the lake for hours. It has been a balm for my soul. For whatever reason, seeing the water again has given me a lift in my spirit, a sense of calm. It is such a beautiful part of God's creation—as I am and as Mikael is. We are all interconnected. I think this is part of the reason why the beauty of the open water brings me this peace right now. Mikael is in a different place than I am, and I can't be where he is at this time, but we are forever connected. Nothing will ever break that bond of love.

MAY 6: AFTER THE FUNERAL

Recent events have had me reflecting on the first few days and weeks after Mikael died. Reliving those days is renewed trauma. I don't think I realized how in shock I was until recently. I recall days of fog and numbness and being on autopilot. I couldn't even cry because I was frozen—my heart, my soul, my brain.

In the first week, as we were preparing for the funeral,

my only focus was on honoring Mikael. Every verse and song chosen. What to say about his life. Every aspect of the day was planned to be a tribute to him. This is where my energy went. After the funeral, when all the activity and planning stopped, I was left feeling at a loss of what to do. After the funeral, when so many others' lives continued on, I was left standing still. As I watched the world continuing around me, I wanted to stop it, to stop everyone and everything because I couldn't keep up.

After the funeral was when the full reality of my loss started to sink in and take hold. It was when the freezing started to come out. I transitioned from numbness to excruciating pain. It was a time when I needed a lot of support, and God made sure I had it. Friends and family continued to check in with me and fill may days with their love and caring. I am forever grateful.

MAY 8: THE CLUB

I have found myself to be a member of a club I never wanted to be a member of. Neither did any of the other members. As a member of this club, I have met some pretty amazing parents, and I would like to tell you about them.

The members of this club are incredibly brave and strong. They find a way to get up every morning, despite their incredible pain, and step forward into all the daily tasks put before them. They step forward every single day.

They are the most compassionate human beings you will find anywhere in the world! Their hearts are filled with love and caring for others. The members of this club have found compassion for others out of their own deep pain and sorrow.

The members in this club have very fragile hearts—hearts that have been shattered and pieced together again.

This may seem to be in opposition to my previous observation about how brave and strong they are, but that is not the case. It is the fragility of their hearts that makes them so brave and awesome. They take their fragile hearts and use them to help others in any way that they can.

These are people who find places to voice their pain where you will never see them. You will not see them sobbing in the sanctuary of their car. You will not know about them lying on the floor of the shower, letting their tears be swept away with the water. You will not see them sitting in the dark of their bedroom, forlorn and bereft. They will not show this to you. They don't wish to burden you. This is the private part of their pain.

The members of this club are some of the finest individuals I have ever met. I wish we were able to be in a club with different membership requirements, but here we are. And I can only say I am honored to know them.

MAY 9: IF

I often think what if
I had an hour with you
What would I say?
What would you say?
Is there anything that
Has been left unsaid?
Or would we just sit
And be together
Side by side
No words required
Absorbing each other's presence
I think we would

MAY 11: FACES OF GRIEF

How easy it is for us to fail to recognize the faces of grief. We expect to see tears, bodies bent over in their pain, pitiful sobbing. This is definitely one of the faces of grief—usually the part we try to keep hidden. However, grief takes so many other forms.

It is the face of the girl at the grocery store checkout, silently unloading her groceries. It is the face of the man sitting on the park bench laughing at something his friend just said to him. It is the couple standing and enjoying the music at a concert. Grief has many expressions and no expression. Sometimes it presents itself outward, but so often it is deafeningly silent. It is not just an emotion that shows up on our faces; it is something we carry as part of our bones, our hearts, our skin. We carry it while we're enjoying time with friends and family, while we do our errands, while we vacation, while we go to work.

I am continually thinking about how I need to keep looking at the faces around me and see what is hidden—to learn the stories and be present for those who need to be seen and heard. I'm often not sure I'm up for the task, and I certainly don't feel confident in my ability, but I know I will try.

MAY 13: MOTHER'S DAY

As Mother's Day approaches, I have found myself dreading it. How do I celebrate being a mother when my son is gone? How do I embrace motherhood? As I lay awake last night thinking, I realized Mother's Day isn't just about me. It is about all the mothers everywhere who love, protect, sacrifice, play, provide, fix, cook, clean, and care. I know I have one of the best mothers in the world. I know I am a good mother, and my sons are terrific people.

Tomorrow I will celebrate my sons, Davis and Mikael.

I will celebrate Davis's heart and kindness and humour and steadfastness.

I will celebrate Mikael's vibrant spirit and giving heart and questioning mind.

I will celebrate my children, hearts of my heart.

Even though Mikael is not here, I can still feel him, and I can celebrate my sons for all they are.

MAY 14: TO MOTHERS

My child,
I need you to know that
I love you with my whole heart.
Your heart is from my heart.
I love you fiercely,
With my entire being,
Ready to protect you like a lion.
I am your lighthouse
To guide you when you're adrift.
My love for you is infinite,
Strong, forgiving, stable.
Nothing you do can change
My everlasting love.
I am sure of you
When you are unsure of yourself.
I see you
With my heart,
With my soul,
With my everything.

MAY 16: OVERWHELMED

I can normally be described as having good coping skills. I am a problem solver and whenever issues arise, I generally take things one step at a time and trust in the Lord to work things out. I have been on an overnight bush trek by myself, just because it was something I wanted to do. Breaking a new snowshoe trail is a lovely winter outing for me. I have completed multiple home renovations over the past years. I once had a friend jokingly tell me that if there were an apocalypse, she would come to my house because I would know how to survive! I'm not sure what happened to that woman. I lose sight of her sometimes.

Yesterday, just as Mother's Day was ending, we discovered our septic tank appears to be leaking. Water is pooling above it, which is not good at all. Then several fuses blew and need to be replaced. This was in addition to some other issues we are dealing with from Mikael's estate and from a rental unit we badly need to sell. Yesterday morning, I woke up feeling so overwhelmed and defeated. I felt like I couldn't cope with these issues. Getting through each day step-by-step takes all my energy, and I just didn't have any emotions left to handle all these extras. Or at least, they felt like extras to me. I was on the verge of tears all day—well, more than on the verge. Tears were shed.

God sent me some reminders yesterday. The reading in my devotions was from 2 Corinthians 1:1-11, and the message was that God doesn't expect me to handle all these things. He wants me to hand it all over to him and allow him to find the pathways and solutions. Later on, my husband phoned me and also reminded me that these issues would work out, and it was so good to just be able to let him do the problem solving.

I am not used to these feelings of helplessness, and I

have found them pretty unsettling. But I suppose being helpless is the best place to be to allow God to take over; I have always found that his solutions are the best ones. This doesn't mean I suddenly don't feel overwhelmed anymore—just that I am working on letting God carry me through.

MAY 18: THE SKUNK

A number of years ago, our neighbour shot a skunk behind a guest cabin on our property in the country. Your first thought may be, "Why would he do such a thing?" and I can tell you, those were my first thoughts too! *Why?* You can imagine the smell of having a skunk carcass less than a hundred meters from the house. Mikael was probably around twelve or thirteen at the time; I don't really remember. What I do remember is realizing the skunk carcass absolutely had to be removed from our property. Mikael and I planned to take a garbage bag, scoop the carcass into it with a shovel, close it, throw it in the back of the truck, then drive way down the road and empty it into the bush.

Well, that's basically how the plan unfolded, plus or minus some details. As bad as the smell was in the yard, we were not prepared for the smell of a dead skunk when we were standing right next to it. It was the most noxious smell you could ever imagine—like we were being gassed! Even with our noses covered, our eyes were streaming with tears. This, of course, made it harder to see, so the process of getting the carcass into the garbage bag took a bit longer than we had intended. But we got it in, tied the bag shut, and tossed it into the back of the truck. We drove down the road and although our original plan had been to dump it out in the bush, there was no way we were opening that bag again! It went into the bush, bag and all.

Anyway, I thought of this memory the other day and

chuckled to myself. Mikael was not a kid you could count on to do the dishes right after supper or put his laundry away, but man, if you had to deal with a dead skunk, he was right there to back you up! He was a good disposal partner, and we definitely had some laughs about it all—after our eyes stopped watering.

Whenever these memories come to mind, I find them to be such a blessing. The memories bring me comfort and keep Mikael close beside me.

MAY 20: UNANTICIPATED FEELINGS

I'm at a women's conference this week. Yesterday morning, I sat in the meeting room listening to a woman talk about her children during the COVID-19 shutdowns and the things they missed out on. I suddenly felt an overwhelming rage. I wanted to scream, *"At least your children are still alive! Get over it!"* I left and went to my room to give myself an emotional break. I am not proud of these feelings, and it is one of the first times I have felt angry. It's difficult to even admit I felt this way. My anger felt so unreasonable, irrational, and vile.

I am normally a very empathetic and compassionate person, so feeling this way is difficult to accept in myself. I usually recognize that every person has their own reality and carries their own difficulties, but that particular morning I just couldn't. I had already spent the night before breaking down in my hotel room with my hands pressed over a picture of Mikael. My eyes were red, and I was emotionally exhausted. I had nothing left.

These are scary feelings for me. I do not ever want to become an angry person or an unfeeling person towards others. I know that is not what God wants for me or what I want for myself. At the same time, I am pretty sure what I felt at that moment was a normal effect of grief, and it is likely there will be times I will feel that way again. How do I cut myself some slack while at the same time ensure that bitterness does not creep into my soul?

I cannot do this without God's help. If I do not stay completely tied to him, I will be lost. And so, I will own these difficult feelings and allow the Lord to soothe them and remind me that I am not alone and that I can release them into his safe hands.

MAY 23: CIRCLING BACK

For the past few days, I have found myself circling back to feelings of disbelief. Once again, I can't get my brain to grasp that this has happened. It doesn't seem like it can possibly be real, that Mikael could be gone. It all just feels so impossible.

I keep hoping to see him pull in and walk across the yard to the house. Or to text me or call me or stop by the office for coffee. I'd like to pretend he's away on a trip somewhere and he'll be back soon. Except he won't. He won't, and I feel utterly frozen.

MAY 25: SOLITARY MOMENTS

I have come to recognize and accept that there will be parts of my journey I have to walk alone. No matter how amazing friends and family are—and they are—the reality is that there are simply times when the complicated enormity of grief is a lonely and solitary burden. During these times, I have come to lean upon several verses that remind me God's promise is to be with me always.

In Matthew 28:20, Jesus said to his disciples, "And surely I am with you always, to the very end of the age." So, when it feels like I'm dropping off the face of the earth some days, I have the certainty that God is with me. Another verse that brings me comfort is Isaiah 41:10, "Do not fear, for I am with you; do not be dismayed, for I am your God. I will strengthen you and help you; I will uphold you with my righteous right hand." This verse helps me visualize God literally putting his hand out for me to rest in and pouring his strength into my body.

My favourite verse has always been Romans 8:38-39: "For I am convinced that neither death nor life, neither angels nor demons, neither the present nor the future, nor any powers, neither height or depth, nor anything else in all creation, will be able to separate us from the love of God that is in Christ Jesus our Lord." I hold onto these promises and the knowledge that I cannot be separated from God's love, even in the times when I am bearing my grief alone.

MAY 26: WHEN BAD THINGS HAPPEN

How many times do we ask the question, "Why do bad things happen to good people?" And when bad things happen specifically to us, we often say, "Why me, God? Why are you doing this to me?"

The thing is, God isn't *doing* anything to us; he is simply not stopping life from happening. All of us, in our humanity, want to avoid pain and suffering. We pray regularly for God to save us, to heal us, to prevent sadness and pain from happening to us and our loved ones. This is a pretty normal human goal, but the problem is that what we really want is heaven on earth. We are not in heaven; we are on earth, and earth is a flawed and damaged place where bad things can and do happen to anyone.

God never promised us that we would not go through terrible hardships or suffering. He did promise us that he would be with us always, to the ends of the earth. I am relying on this promise each and every day.

MAY 27: PLANS

I am retiring as of June 30. So many people have asked, "Are you counting down the days?" "Are you excited?" "Do you have any plans?"

The thing is, nothing about my retirement feels normal. I would like to be excited, but this is a feeling I don't really recognize lately. I look forward to things, definitely, but excitement feels a bit out of reach for me right now. Honestly, what I think I will feel the most when June 30 rolls around is relief. Blessed relief!

And as to plans? I made plans before Mikael died. I envisioned him in my plans. Now, making plans seems so fleeting and untrustworthy. I no longer have the vision of my retirement that I had before I started living in the After. Sure, I have some home renovation work for the next year, but those are really just short-term jobs to be done; they aren't really plans. And yes, those jobs will occupy me for the first bit that I am retired, and that is a good thing. But long-term plans? I really just don't think I know how to do that anymore. I find myself very fluid right now; I'll decide on things as they come. And I think that is okay.

MAY 30: IN MEMORY

This past weekend, I began planting Mikael's garden. It is a work in progress, and I will add to it gradually as the current plants settle themselves in and spread out. It is a beautiful spot for the bench that was given to me by a group of friends. It has been very therapeutic to spend time working in the soil and watching the garden develop.

The garden is one more symbol of the memory of Mikael. Like the bracelet I wear, the tattoo on my arm, his clothes that I've kept, the picture wall. Honouring Mikael's memory in all these ways is what I will continue to do.

These symbols I've been creating, gathering, and adding to are an outward expression of my love for him. They stem from the fierce and constant love in my heart for my sweet child.

I found out the other day that good friends of Mikael's just had their baby, and they used Mikael's name as one of the middle names of their little boy. They did this as a way to keep his memory alive forever. I simply don't have the words to describe how much this means to me. When I heard about it, all I could do was sob. Tears of such gratitude and sweet sorrow.

I believe keeping the memory of our children alive is one of the most important things for grieving parents. We don't want anyone to forget about them. When friends and family honor Mikael's memory in these tangible ways, I can only hope they know how much it touches my heart to the deepest core and how much I love them for what they are doing.

CHAPTER 6

june

JUNE 1: HOW

How is it that I feel nothing
and everything at the same time.
The frozenness of my mind
unable to break the surface for air.
And yet, I'm flooded
with the intensity of longing.
Longing,
excruciating, never-ending longing.
It is a welling up of
the most tender and deepest love
with nowhere to put it,
creating a sensation of paralysis.
Perhaps that is how
my mind protects me.

JUNE 3: HUNKERED DOWN

Some days I simply feel so shattered that I can't find it in me to interact with others unless I absolutely have to. There are days when my body feels like a husk. I am like the brittle leaves in the fall, being scuttled along the ground by the wind. On these days, God and I hunker down together and endure. I read his Word, listen to music, look at pictures, sit and look out at the lake, and focus on just being. It is necessary to do this. There will just be days like this, and trying to make yourself "soldier on" when it happens is detrimental in the long run.

The best thing I can do when these days come—and they will—is to let them. To sit in them. To be in them. To acknowledge them and not feel guilty about my lack of productivity. And, really, there is productivity in these days; it is just a very quiet, slow trickle of healing movement only God and I may notice.

JUNE 6: ASHES

On Saturday, we buried Mikael's ashes. We chose a spot on my parents' property on Lake of the Woods and planted a lilac tree as a memorial to him. I will add a stone once I get it engraved. It is a beautiful spot and something we needed to be able to do as a family. Even though I know Mikael is not here, that he is with the Lord doing amazing things, I still felt a sense of completeness knowing that his ashes have a resting place that is meaningful to our family. I guess it is something about grief that these tangible things bring comfort and significance. It makes sense, because when those we love are gone, we need to have something physical to touch and see.

I went out on Friday to prepare the spot. I know I could have asked for help to do this, but I just wanted to do this part on my own. I needed to be able to do this for Mikael. There was a lot of clay in the location, so the digging was pretty darn difficult! I chopped, dug, shoveled, rested, repeated. I needed to dig a hole large enough for good, black earth and fertilizer, one that would allow the tree's roots to settle and spread. As I slogged away, I realized one of God's gifts to me is very clearly tenacity!

At home we have a pizza oven we built, and it happens to need another coating of clay mixture to patch a few cracks. I had been thinking about where we would get the clay that we needed. Digging the hole for Mikael's tree provided all the clay necessary! A resting place for Mikael's ashes brought me a sense of comfort, a realization of the spirit of tenacity, and the clay needed for the oven. It's funny how God works things out that way.

JUNE 8: THE NONVERBAL RESPONSES

In the past several weeks, there have been a couple of times when someone I don't know very well has asked me how

Mikael died. Each time I felt my stomach clench, my breath catch, and a sense of high alert as I watched their faces when I said the words "accidental overdose." Because, you see, verbal responses and nonverbal responses are two very different things. As the mother of a child with the disease of addiction, I have become very in tune to the nonverbal reactions of people when this is the topic. So, while I hear the words, "I'm sorry for your loss," I'm also looking for the nonverbal cues that indicate either understanding and compassion or judgement and pity.

The truth is, in my experience, there are parents out there who truly believe their child would never become an addict because they are better parents. There is still a stigma that addiction is a personality flaw as opposed to an actual disease that no one ever wishes to have. I have sensed the judgement of those who think having a relapse is a result of just not trying hard enough. The truth is, there are people who suffer from the disease of addiction that survive, and there are those who do not. Just like there are those who survive other illnesses and those who do not. It has nothing to do with how hard anyone has tried.

In the past years, as a mother of a child with the disease of addiction, I have learned to hold close to me the fabulous friends who understand and support us. I have learned not to spend my time or energy on trying to forge relationships with those who are not able to. And, if you are reading this and you are struggling as a parent whose beautiful child has the disease of addiction, this mother bear is in your corner!

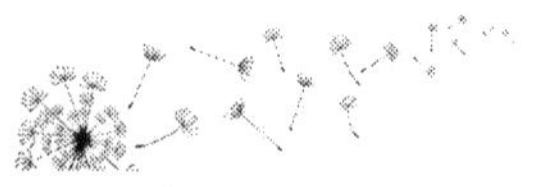

JUNE 10: SOMEDAY

Someday.
The problem with someday
is that it's not
today.
Someday is hopeful
and yet unknown.
Someday is better than never.
Someday has a future
but someday is not today.
And I don't know how many todays
there will be without you until
someday comes.

JUNE 12: HIDDEN BEAUTY

On Saturday morning I walked from my hotel to Tim Horton's along Airport Road in Toronto. Anyone who has stayed in the area knows that Airport Road is not in the least picturesque. Noise, traffic, dirt, garbage. As I walked back with my coffee, though, I noticed these beautiful little pink and white flowers growing everywhere in the grass alongside the sidewalk. They were so dainty and pretty. It reminded me that beauty can be found anywhere.

I started thinking about how we sometimes have ugliness in our lives—parts of us we're not so proud of or terrible life events. Beauty can still survive if we can look around to see it. I thought about Mikael and how, despite dealing with the disease of addiction, there was so much beauty in him, in his heart for others, in his sincerity, in his laughter. He shone so brightly for those who took the time to see it and to know him.

In my own life, as I continue to walk through the loss of him, I know I can still find beauty. The strength of friendships, the love of friends and family, the sparkling of sun on the water, the growth in my garden. And I can focus on cultivating the beautiful parts of who I am and let God take over the ugly parts.

JUNE 15: BIRTHDAY GIFT

When the kids were young and in school, I saved some of their precious artwork and kept it in a box Mikael made years later in high school shop class. The boys would take the box out from time to time, and we'd go through the artwork within. We'd have a chuckle at the stick figures, the round bodies with arms and legs sticking out, and enjoy a trip down memory lane. I think it meant a lot to both Davis and Mikael that I saved these pieces of their childhood.

Unbeknownst to me, my sister had my daughter-in-law, Carollyn, go through them and find a piece that had a message from Mikael. She had a necklace made with his message, in his writing, and gave it to me for my birthday. Oh my heart! Such a gift! I have been wearing it since. Having his words around my neck is such a special feeling.

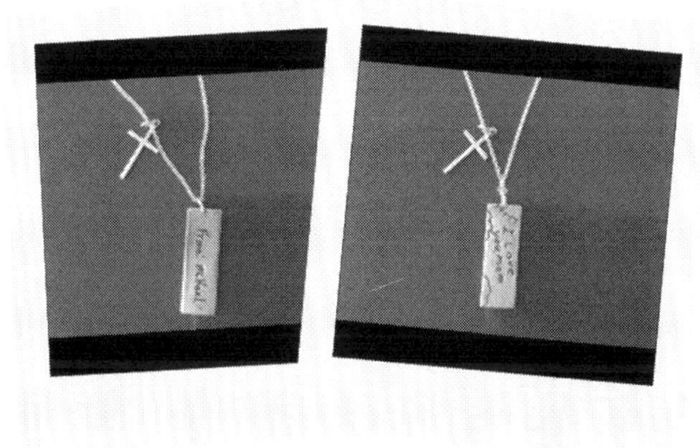

JUNE 17: ENDURANCE

My morning devotions over the past few days have been from the book of Job. I wasn't sure how they would go, but I have to say that overall, I've found them helpful and thought-provoking. Today's devotional mentioned the idea of endurance several times: learning from the endurance of Job, how enduring suffering allows us to bring comfort to others, and the concept of who is watching us endure. I started to think about what endurance actually meant, so I looked it up.

Two definitions came up. One, to suffer patiently—and the second, to remain in existence, to last. I'm not entirely sure I'm suffering patiently. Suffering, yes. Patiently? I'm not sure I feel either patient or impatient. It's not like I'm stuck in a traffic jam for hours and am patiently waiting. I'm in an endless reality of grief that won't go away. I'm not angry. I still trust my Lord. Does that mean I'm enduring? I suppose there's not really a choice, but I do think we can endure something many different ways. Because if the second definition is to remain in existence, or to last, we can do that in bitterness and anger or we can do it in love, trust, and compassion. I hope I can keep choosing to endure with love.

This thinking brings me to the last part of my devotions, which talked about who is watching us endure. I realize many people are, in fact, watching me endure. The thing is, losing Mikael has been horrific, excruciating, painful, and full of so, so, so much sorrow. But I also know God uses everything we experience to help others. I know he can provide strength to me, he will carry me, and that if I continue to fully trust him, he will use all of this to help others.

Do I wish I could be helpful to others some other way? I sure do! But I'm here, and I'm not alone here. There are others with me, enduring, and God is with me making sure I do too. Even though there have been—and will be—dark days, I can endure with love because I have a relationship with Christ built on his love for me and his gift of salvation.

JUNE 21: IRELAND

I am home from spending just over a week in Ireland. It is such a magical and beautiful place with absolutely spectacular scenery. It is both rugged and quaint. It was a well-needed getaway. I found myself thinking about Mikael everywhere we went, and I felt him with me so strongly on this trip. He would have been fascinated by the Giant's Causeway and the theories and stories of how it was formed. He just might have run into the frigid water at the beach, just to say he went swimming in Ireland! He would have loved the history and the fact that almost everywhere you go, there is an old ruin in the middle of a town or field.

But the Book of Kells! I think he might have swooned. The actual presence of such an ancient book and the chronology of how it was written and came to be at Trinity College would have completely captured his imagination. The stunningly decorated pages would have put him in awe! As I wandered through the exhibit, I could picture his reactions, comments, and questions, making the experience even more memorable and special for me.

I am so very thankful for this experience.

JUNE 23: IDENTITY

I have been struggling a bit with my identity since Mikael died. Such a huge part of my identity is as a mom. Being a mom isn't *what* I am, it is *who* I am. I know people say our identities are so much more than that; that who we are is about how we think, what we're good at, what we're not good at, our personal philosophies, and so on. Well, I can acknowledge this as true, but I am a fiercely loving mother; that is who I am. I am Davis's mom, and I am Mikael's mom, and I have poured every ounce of who I am into being their mom and loving them with my heart and soul. Now, it feels like a big chunk of who I am has been cut out of me.

I also know there will be those who remind me that I should be finding my identity in the Lord. That is not the issue though; it never has been. I know who I am in the Lord. It is my "momness" that is floundering. I love Mikael and Davis bigger than the sky, but Mikael is not physically here, and it feels like my love for him has nowhere to go. It's being sent out into the air, into space, to another realm, and part of my motherhood is being sent with it. And no, I can't just refocus this love on someone else because it is love specifically for Mikael. I have tons of love for others, but this love is only for him.

I believe that over time, God will help me work through this and come to a place with my mom identity restored. In time. Right now, it is a painful process of struggling and learning and figuring out.

JUNE 25: SORROW

Sorrow—
What does it mean?
Is it sadness?
I suppose it is partly.
But sorrow goes deeper—
deeper into your bones.
Sorrow takes up residence,
soaking into your being.
But sorrow has a partner;
that is love.

For the measure of sorrow
is equal to the measure of love
that created it.
Sorrow cannot be
without love.
Remember as you carry sorrow
that you are also carrying love.
And while sorrow
has seeped into your body,
it is surrounded and protected
by love.

JUNE 27: HATEFUL DISEASE

Those that regularly read my blog must sometimes wonder why my entries can fluctuate from hopeful to despair over the matter of a few days. That is just the nature of this journey. Lately, I have been rather consumed with how much I hate the disease of addiction. *Hate, hate, hate it!* This disease robbed Mikael of so much: his self-esteem, peace, his security, family times, relationships, sleep, his health, and ultimately his life. This disease robbed our family of Mikael's time, peace of mind, and his presence in our lives. This insidious disease creeps its way into families with intent to destroy. This disease can strike anyone, anytime, and is always waiting in the shadows—even when its victim is recovering and doing well.

I find that all my anger is directed towards the disease of addiction. I am not angry at God; he did not cause Mikael to have this disease. I'm angry at the disease itself for taking Mikael from us and sending us into the After where none of us wanted to be.

As I feel this anger percolate in my body, I know I will

have to direct it somewhere useful: particularly in fighting this disease. I know I can't just let the anger sit there because that will harm me in the end and, once again, let this disease have a victory. So, I will somehow turn my thoughts to what actions I can take that can support those suffering from this disease in a positive way. I don't yet know what that will look like for me, and I find myself waiting for God's direction and hoping that I am listening when he provides it.

JUNE 30: MY DREAM

A few nights ago, Mikael was in my dream. I was walking along a path with a lot of other people with no idea of where we were going. As we were walking, we came upon a group of children, each sitting on a cot. The other people kept walking, but I stopped to visit with the kiddos. I spent some time talking to them, and they told me there was another path that branched off near them. I decided to take that path instead. It was a path that went through the countryside.

As I walked onward, I was joined by Tim, then Davis and my granddaughters, and then Carollyn. We all kept walking together towards a destination we weren't sure of, but we all seemed to know it would be a good place. Then Mikael came walking towards us from further ahead. It was so amazing to see him! He gave me a big hug and walked with us for a bit. I remember feeling so warm inside as we all walked side by side.

Then he turned to me and told me he had to go on ahead—he had work to do—but we would find him when we arrived at our destination. He walked ahead of us and gradually disappeared.

In the past seven months, I have been yearning to see Mikael in my dreams. This was the first time. It was so comforting and reassuring to see him and receive his message that we would find him again when we reach our destination.

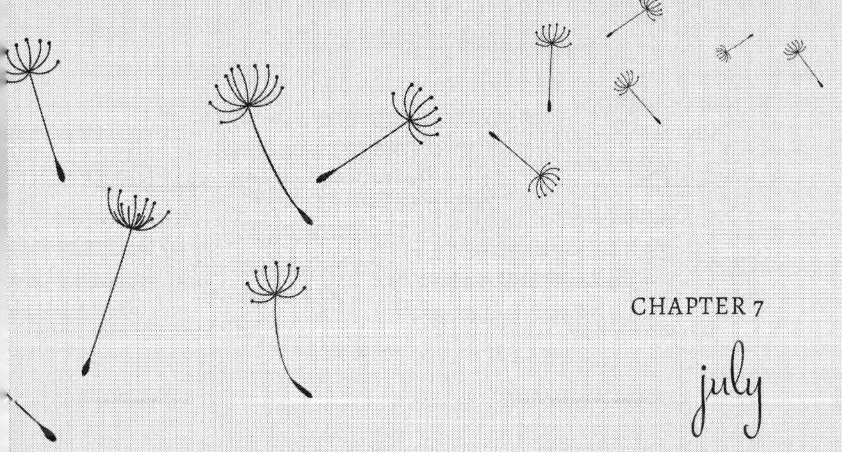

CHAPTER 7

july

JULY 1: PEACE

How often do we all wish for peace? And what kind of peace is it that we need and hope for? Of course, there is the "Kids, stop yelling and fooling around so I can sit and enjoy my cup of coffee" kind of peace. There is also a deep, inner peace we feel in our souls. This peace is often mistaken for the feeling we have when we are not experiencing any strife or hardship. This is not so. Peace is not the absence of difficulty; it is the knowledge of being held and cared for despite difficulty. Knowing that God is carrying us and walking alongside us is what brings us to the state of inner peace in our souls.

Having this kind of peace doesn't mean we are not also feeling pain; it simply means that we know God understands our pain and is with us in it. This kind of peace requires faith. It requires the faith to believe God is who he says he is, and that he will do what he says he will do. Peace requires faith in our salvation and faith in the knowledge of God's love for us. It is faith in the unseen.

I say this because I know the only way I have found any peace amidst my grief and loss is the peace I have found in the Lord—in knowing he loves me and cares for me and is right beside me in my pain. It is a peace I am so very grateful for, and I know I could not have it without God's presence in my life.

JULY 3: ABSENCE

Your absence is felt like a solid presence.
During family gatherings, I can feel the lack of
your voice, your laughter.
You are so noticeably missing,
a gaping hole in the family garment.
As I join the gathering,
chatting and laughing,
playing with the kids,
I can feel your absence under my skin,
an ache in my heart.
An ache I'm coming to accept
as a natural part of me.
It is silently carried.
The quiet introspection is saved for the ride home,
when I can process the ache
from your absence
where no one can see
the evidence on my face.

JULY 5: IN THE PIT AGAIN

The past few days have felt very much like, "I don't want this to be my life. I don't want to do this. I don't want to feel this anymore." Except I have no choice. I find myself in the pit once again. The excruciating pain of missing Mikael. The guilt over what I could have done better as a mom. The agony of the long wait before I see my son again.

This brings me to two thought processes. One is something I have probably flogged over and over, but I think it is important that this concept is understood. As grieving parents, we often look and act like we are doing okay. We do not put our agony out there for everyone to see. We tend to express it only in our private moments. So, what you see is a person who is going about their business, attending work, attending family and friend functions, talking, laughing, participating. And we want to do all those things. But underneath is the constant absence of our child. It never goes away. There is nothing you can do about this; I simply want you all to be aware that this is what is actually happening when you see us in public and spend time with us. You can't change it, but please don't make the mistake of thinking we are doing great and are getting past our tragedy. We are not. We are simply learning to live around it.

The other thought I have is the one about peace I wrote about a few days ago. When I am in the pit of despair, it is the one thing I have to cling on to: the peace of knowing God is with me in this pit. The only place I know to go to when I have these "bottom of the well" days is the foot of the cross. Where else can I go? There is no one on this earth who knows me the way God knows me. I need him even more than I need air to breathe. When I am face-down on the floor, feeling such pain, all I can do is call out to him to help me.

There are days where I just feel so tired. Tired of being strong. Tired of getting out of bed. Tired of dealing with other people. Incapable of finishing tasks. Just tired. Weary. You might think, where is the peace in this? It is in being able to just let it be, to hand it over to the Lord and ride the waves with him through this.

JULY 7: PROCESSING FEELINGS

My mom passed away on Tuesday, and I find myself trying to process a tangle of feelings. Mom had dementia and had declined over the years, and I've known over the past month that she was not going to be here much longer. Because her memory gradually disappeared, I've had a gradual grieving process. Over time, I've felt the loss of not being able to talk to her about things anymore, the loss of parts of her personality, and the changes in her demeanour. I've known the grief of watching her frustration as her brain failed her.

Even though I was prepared for her to die, and I know she is now with the Lord in paradise, I still feel sad. But it is a confused sadness, because it is all mixed up with the sadness I already feel with Mikael's loss. It's like my sadness cup was already overflowing, and then more was poured into it, and it has nowhere to go but to just spill out everywhere. It's all a bit of a jumble to me, and I'm trying to sort through it.

Are there two separate grieving processes, or is it now all one together? In a way, I do feel a bit like I'm holding two separate griefs in my head and heart. I'm honestly not sure, but I guess that's okay. I can take whatever time I need to let all these feelings sort themselves out in my mind.

JULY 9: GAME FACE

I was prepared but not prepared for how tired I would be today after Mom's funeral. I knew the day would exhaust me, but I don't think I appreciated to what extent. Anyone reading this who has planned and attended the funeral of a loved one knows the exhaustion I am talking about. It all adds up: the planning, the task of writing an obituary and a eulogy, the raw emotion of reading it to those in attendance and listening in turn to the heartfelt sharing of your siblings, the navigation of a social gathering. In addition, carrying grief on grief takes a lot of energy. What I now understand is that it takes even more energy than I realized to maintain your "game face," which is of course exactly what we do in social circumstances, funerals especially.

I know I have developed the habit of putting on my "game face" in most social gatherings. When I am asked how I am, my general response is "not bad" or "doing okay." And I also know this is a pretty standard response from other grieving parents as well. Why do we do this?

I think there are several reasons that I respond this way:

1. I don't want to break down and cry in public. If I start, I'm terrified that I will sob uncontrollably.
2. I really don't want to hear any useless platitudes, which, in large social gatherings, may very well happen.
3. I honestly don't want to inflict my pain on one of my friends or family and have their day pulled into the agony of mine.
4. I just don't have the words to describe how I might be feeling or the energy to try sometimes.

A funeral is most definitely a social gathering. Most of the time, you will notice that the bereaved family seems so together and strong. They navigate the day with seeming grace and serenity, shedding few if any tears, holding themselves together. People will make comments such as, "Your strength is amazing" or "I don't know how you do it."

Well, I'm pretty sure I wasn't the only one with my "game face" on yesterday. I feel, in fact, quite certain that my brother and two sisters had theirs on as well, for all the same reasons that I did.

What I want to say to them is that I truly feel and understand what you are feeling. All of it.

JULY 11: GUILT REVISITED

I feel the need to return to the topic of guilt. It is probably the most difficult struggle in my spiritual life. I struggled with guilt before Mikael died and even more so after. All the mistakes I made as his momma can come crashing around me on any given day. It is a definite spiritual battle. I often wonder if it is for most people because guilt is so easy to slip into. Guilt is an insidious enemy not to be confused with conviction. Conviction is a true, sincere, knowledge of having done wrong and taking the steps with God to seek forgiveness and correct the wrong. Guilt is based on lies and fear. Unlike conviction, guilt is a destructive force with the sole purpose of robbing us of our peace and joy. It leads us into faulty decisions with often painful outcomes. Conviction comes from the Holy Spirit. Guilt does not.

When I experience an onslaught of guilty feelings, I have learned to start talking to God immediately. It is my best defence. Taking all these harmful feelings to God and breaking them apart into accurate facts versus lies helps me to pull myself back to reality. Focusing on God's Word as truth and not my own faulty thinking pulls me out of the brambles and sets me back on the path. If you struggle with feelings of guilt in your journey as I do, I want to offer you understanding and encouragement and hope.

JULY 13: WHERE DO I FIND YOU

Where do I find you?
Oh, in places both expected and unexpected!
I find you in the in-between place in the car on my drive home. When I can just let go and think about you and sift through memories.
I find you in a song that comes on my playlist. One of your favorites. Of course, that's why I downloaded it! I think about why you liked it so much, and the music tugs at my soul and connects me with you.
In the quiet of a morning or afternoon on the deck, contemplating the sun on the water and letting my thoughts drift to you and all that you are.
I find you in the laughter at a family gathering. How you loved to laugh! How I love to hear the laughter of others to fill the gap of missing yours!
I find you first thing in the morning, as I open my eyes and look for your picture. I end my day in the same way. Just saying "Hey there" and then "Goodnight."
You can be found, unexpectedly, when I am expressing irritation, quietly telling me to sit back for a moment.
Most definitely, you can be found in the memory of

pictures that I keep everywhere, all around me,
of every moment of your life.
Your voice can be heard in your messages and videos
on my phone.
In the moments of peace, where my heart rests, you
are there, in the silence, letting me know that
rest is needed.
And, if I'm really lucky, you can be found in my
dreams, where you are so real and for those
brief, subconscious moments, you are almost
here.

JULY 21: MEMORIES AND BUSYNESS

Over the past week, I have been working nonstop on our rental house as we prepare it to sell. During the day, I am so busy with all the tasks needing to be done that I am not focusing on my grief so much. However, on the ride home, and while relaxing in the evening, all my memories and thoughts come flooding in. I feel the loss of Mikael's presence in our lives and cherish memories of him. What have I learned this week? Work and busyness can be helpful in providing our brains with other things to focus on, but they cannot be used as a total escape from our feelings. Being productive is a positive thing when there is a balance and we allow ourselves to feel what we need to. I continue to learn as I travel this road and navigate the very complex moving pieces of grief.

JULY 23: MY GRACE IS SUFFICIENT

I remember Paul talking about having a burden God did not take from him. He never says exactly what it is, and there is much speculation about what kind of condition he had. It doesn't really matter what it was; the point really is that God told him his grace is sufficient.

> Even if I should choose to boast, I would not be a fool, because I would be speaking the truth. But I refrain, so no one will think more of me than is warranted by what I do or say, or because of these surpassingly great revelations. Therefore, in order to keep me from becoming conceited, I was given a thorn in my flesh, a messenger of Satan, to torment me. Three times I pleaded with the Lord to take it away from me. But he said to me, "My grace is sufficient for you, for my power is made perfect in weakness." Therefore I will boast all the more gladly about my weaknesses, so that Christ's power may rest on me. That is why, for Christ's sake, I delight in weaknesses, in insults, in hardships, in persecutions, in difficulties. For when I am weak, then I am strong.
>
> 2 Corinthians 12:6-10

God's power is made evident when we give him our weaknesses. My weakness is my grief, and I do not have to bear it alone. God's grace is sufficient. I know there will be times when it doesn't feel like that for me, and yet it is still so. Even when I may not be feeling it, God's grace will still be present.

God's grace involves so many levels of who he is. He is the God of comfort, and I have access to all his power and love when I feel like I'm not enough or I can't go on. God sent Jesus to us, and he loved us so much he died for us. Jesus died for me, and I find strength and hope at the foot of the cross every day. This journey of grief is one in which I need constant guidance and direction, and the Holy Spirit is here to do just that for me. God in all his forms is sufficient grace.

CHAPTER 8
final thoughts

I want to share some of the things I have found helpful to me on this road. If any of them are helpful to you, I am glad.

I cannot make it one single step without God's help.

My faith is instrumental in my being able to get out of bed some mornings. I don't say this lightly, and I am well aware that we often get hit with platitudes about faith from those who have no inkling about what we are dealing and coping with. For me, reading God's Word and allowing God to carry and guide me is what I need to do. To be clear, when I say God is helping me, I don't mean my pain is magically relieved; it is here in all its horrificness, every single day. What God does is help me take one step and then another, and God can be counted on to be with me in the bottom of the well every time I sink there.

I let my friends and family support me in every way they are able.

Having people I love check in on me, visit with me, read my blog, give me a call, etc. has given me the boost I need some days to keep going. It's okay to reach out to family and friends and let them know you are having an excruciating day, down in the pit, and you need some support. My husband is an amazing and compassionate supporter for whom I am forever grateful.

When we were planning Mikael's funeral, I was in such an emotional fog. I had scratched out ideas for what we wanted in a notebook but really wasn't capable of planning my way out of a paper bag at that point. I handed my chicken scratch to my younger sister, who is an amazing organizer, and she just did it. Everyone helped. It was beautiful. It's okay to ask for help.

I connected with other parents who were experiencing the same loss.

In particular, one good friend who also lost her son has been such an amazing support for me, and I hope I am for her too. It is so important to be able to talk to at least one other person who knows exactly what you are thinking and feeling without any

explanations.

I give myself at least one task to do every day. Sometimes it's a simple task, like doing the dishes or changing the water filter, and sometimes I choose more complicated tasks, like a bit of home renovating. I admit I am terrified of becoming depressed, so making sure I get up each day and accomplish one thing is important to me. It doesn't mean I don't take time to rest and just sit with my grief; I do that too. Doing at least one thing every day helps me to feel that I am still part of this world.

Listening to music has been comforting and soothing for me.

I listen to songs that I connect with and that Mikael connected with. For me, music allows an emotional release.

Spending time with friends and family is important to me. It can become very easy to isolate and insulate ourselves because it feels like no one understands what is happening to us. Even though that may be true, our friends and family want to support us, and taking part in the world around us keeps us from self-destruction. I especially love spending time with my son Davis, his wife Carollyn, and our granddaughters Gwenyth (age four) and Roslyn (age two). Being with the girls is such a joy, and I find that they unknowingly soothe my grief with their conversation and antics.

Activities requiring full concentration provide me with a mental respite from my constantly churning brain.

Because I think about Mikael all the time, I need to have these reprieves to rest my mind. A sewing job or a puzzle are examples of activities I find keep my mind fully occupied and provide this much-needed rest. It's important to find a balance between time spent processing my grief and time spent occupying my mind on other things in order to give it a rest.

There are days where I simply need to sit with my feelings.

It took me some time to give myself permission to do this, but it is necessary. I especially need to do this in the mornings. Each morning starts with the realization that Mikael is gone, and I need time to gather myself and mentally prepare for the rest of the day. I also had to give myself permission to let the days where I am at the bottom of the pit to just happen and to not try to change them.

Spending time outdoors is a balm for my soul.

It allows me to think more clearly and focus on positive memories of Mikael. Time that I spend outside, on the lake, in the garden, snowshoeing, walking or sliding with my grandchildren provide me with such positive energy. It also brings me into touch with God's wonder of creation and reminds me that he is sovereign.

In closing, I want to thank you for reading my journal entries, and I hope that sharing my journey so far has been helpful to you. Losing one of your children is something no parent is prepared for, and regardless of how you have lost your child, I firmly believe you will very likely be suffering from trauma as well. I know I did. It is imperative that we face the trauma we are experiencing so we can continue stepping forward each day as we learn to grow around our grief and sorrow. We may need help talking about and processing any trauma we have experienced, and God will provide the resources we need. I believe the new way of living in the After cannot be done without the Lord's help.

There are days of excruciating pain, days of emptiness, days of sorrow and confusion. There are also days with laughter and joy, and these days are a gift and necessary for us to build strength on this journey. I hope you know it is okay to feel joy and happiness, and that these positive feelings can coexist along with our grief. These positive feelings will help us with our grief. For my part, I plan to keep working on my own growth and ask God to keep steering the boat I am in.

afterword

One thing I wish to touch on is the need for those of us who are grieving to connect with fellow grievers. I highly recommend finding a grief support group either in person or online. The one that I am currently a part of is called Grief Share, and my husband and I are facilitating it at our church. It is a thirteen-week grief support group and more information can be found about it on griefshare.org.

I have also seen other grief support groups online through Facebook but haven't linked to them, so I am not able to comment on what they are like. The important thing is that you find a group that works for you and meets your needs.

In my opinion, there are two crucial things in a grief support group. One is that all members of the group are suffering from grief due to the death of a loved one. (I say this because there are many other forms of grief due to things like job loss, divorce, etc.).

The other is that the group is facilitated in such a way that members are able to share practical strategies and ideas for living day to day with grief. We need to have these positive building blocks of support in order to continue growing and healing.

acknowledgments

I have many people to thank for encouraging me and for helping me get this book through the publishing process.

First I would like to thank Jennifer, Brooke, and Morgan from Tandem Services Ink for all their help in the editing and publishing process. I would have been floundering on my own for sure. Their assistance and guidance have been instrumental in getting this book into publishable form.

Many thanks go to Stephanie Feger and her team at emPower PR for such a beautiful cover design.

I am so very thankful for my family and friends who have supported me and encouraged me to write this book. I am particularly thankful for my husband and best friend, Tim, who is always there for me and who believes in me when I don't always believe in myself. Carollyn, for your constant love and encouragement. It goes without saying, but I'll say it anyway, how thankful I am for my sons Davis and Mikael. Davis, you have been such a support to me, always looking out for me despite your own deep grief. Mikael, we miss you so very much, and I am so grateful for you just being you and for the time I was given to be able to spend with you here on this earth.

I am so grateful to my Lord and Saviour for his love and comfort and for holding me in his righteous right hand.

about the author

Leanne Davidson lives with her husband, Tim, in her hometown of Kenora, Ontario. She has a bachelor of science degree and a bachelor of education degree. She spent twenty-five years as a teacher and then as a union representative for the Ontario English Catholic Teachers Association and is now retired.

Leanne loves to be outdoors in the beauty of northwestern Ontario, where she lives and spends much of her time boating and gardening in the summer and snowshoeing in the winter. *A Beautiful Pain* is her first published book. She is currently working on two other books; one is a compilation of her poetry and the other is a Christian devotional for grievers.

Leanne can be contacted via email at kenoralake4@gmail.com or through her blog website: amothersgriefjourney.com.

Manufactured by Amazon.ca
Bolton, ON